Singers of the New Song

Other books by George A. Maloney, S.J.
published by Ave Maria Press:

ALONE WITH THE ALONE

PRAYER OF THE HEART

THE EVERLASTING NOW

GEORGE A. MALONEY, S.J.

Singers of the New Song

A Mystical Interpretation of the Song of Songs

AVE MARIA PRESS
Notre Dame, Indiana

Acknowledgments:

Sincere thanks to Mrs. Rita Ruggiero for typing this manuscript and to Sister Joseph Agnes for her careful reading and correcting of the manuscript.

Grateful acknowledgment is made to Darton, Longman & Todd, Ltd., and Doubleday & Company, Inc., N.Y., for excerpts from *The Jerusalem Bible*, ©1966 by the same. Unless otherwise noted, all scriptural texts are from this Bible version.

Thanks to ICS Publications for excerpts from *The Collected Works of St. John of the Cross* translated by Kieran Kavanaugh and Otilio Rodriguez. ICS Publications, 2131 Lincoln Road, N.E., Washington, D.C. 20002 1979.

Imprimi Potest: Rev. Joseph A. Novak, S.J.
                  Provincial of the New York Province

Library of Congress Catalog Card Number: 85-71639

International Standard Book Number: 0-87793-291-3 (Cloth)
                                            0-87793-292-1 (Paper)

Cover and text design by Elizabeth J. French

Printed and bound in the United States of America

To Dr. Jean O'Donnell
and
Dr. Patricia Jersin
who have learned the wisdom
of becoming like little children

TABLE OF CONTENTS

Introduction

This is a book about God's passionate love for us as revealed in Jesus Christ. The core of Jesus' revelation to his disciples—the revelation he went to his death to prove—is that "the Father himself loves you for loving me and believing that I came from God" (Jn 16:27). "God is love" (1 Jn 4:8) is the summation of the Christian message.

But do we truly believe that God loves you and me, both individually and corporately? We can readily give an intellectual assent to such a truth. But part of our understanding of God's supreme fullness of being is to withdraw any *passion* from his love for us. God, we believe, loves us but in a giving, not receiving, way. He is perfect, complete and independent of us. He needs no one. He gives his love in a dispassionate manner to us. In a word, we really don't believe God truly empties himself in Jesus Christ for love of us and truly desires our return of love.

From scripture we see God as personal and involved, full of desire to be discovered by us human beings in every sunset, flower of the field, in sheep. "Yahweh my God, how great you are! Clothed in majesty and glory, wrapped in a robe of light!" (Ps 104:1). But his deepest presence as love is communicated by him to us directly at all times in our human situation and especially when we love one another. "I have loved you with an everlasting love, so I am constant in my affection for you" (Jer 31:3). "As long as we love one another God will live in us" (1 Jn 4:12).

Bridal Mysticism

There are many metaphors and allegories in scripture and devotional writings which are used to describe the God-man's relationship to us human beings. He is the Good Shepherd who feeds and protects us. He is the Good Samaritan who binds up our wounds and sees to our healing. He is a king, all-powerful, and we are his servants. He is the vinedresser who protects his vines from the little foxes, but who also prunes the vines for greater fruit. He is a judge who can sentence us to an eternal life of bliss or pain.

But one image that predominates is that of God as the lover of humanity, the great *philanthropos* of the human race. Jesus is the image of the invisible God (Col 1:15), and he best mirrors the perfection of God as lover when he dies for love of us. Is it any wonder that the most consistent and powerful metaphor used in scripture to describe God's burning love for his people and for each individual who enters into the kingdom of heaven is that of God, and, above all, Christ as the bridegroom?

We read in the Old Testament, especially after the exile when God renewed his covenant, how God is the bridegroom and his chosen people are his bride. He does not make a contract so much as a covenant based on self-emptying love and intimate concern for his people. Hosea is the prophet of such an espousal:

> I will betroth you to myself for ever,
> betroth you with integrity and justice,
> with tenderness and love;
> I will betroth you to myself with faithfulness,
> and you will come to know Yahweh (Hos 2:21-22).

Isaiah beautifully describes such an intimate, bridal relationship between God and his people, Israel:

> Like a young man marrying a virgin,
> so will the one who built you wed you,
> and as the bridegroom rejoices in his bride,
> so will your God rejoice in you (Is 62:5).

But the peak of bridal mysticism is found in the beautiful *Song of Songs* of the Old Testament. It can be read and prayerfully experienced on various levels. Most Jewish and Christian commentators have pointed out that the *literal* meaning of this collection of love poems describes in very concrete and sensuous terms the beauty and passion of human love between a man and a woman. Such a description of faithful and happy, passionate human love points also to the corresponding characteristics of divine love as the fulfillment of that which we see in human love.

Speaking of God

But how does one speak of God's passionate love, not only for all his human children, but also for the unique individual persons that you and I are? He has spoken in the prose and poetry of the Old and New Testaments. God continues to speak to us in our own individual prayerful encounters with him and in our communal liturgical prayer. And basic to such language used is *symbolism*. Through symbolism, as Carl Jung often pointed out, in all cultures and in all times God and humanity meet.

In our Western world, however, the ability to move beyond the merely literal meaning of a text of scripture to penetrate to other, more hidden levels of meaning and experience has become very difficult for most of us. To feel comfortable with religious symbols is an art that requires cultivation on our part. Through symbolism, words and reality acquire a deeper and more subtle direction than they normally convey. Through symbols we are able to rise above the limitations of an "objective" world to look somewhat into the face of God himself. Symbols allow us human beings to enter into God's real world and to participate in his love and beauty.

Theology will always be in tension, experiencing imperfections, and constantly reaching to purify the inadequacies of human language in order to encounter more intimately God as loving gift.

Various Interpretations

When we approach a writing of scripture such as the *Song of Songs*, which is so brimming with symbols, we become easily confused as to the "correct" interpretation. The great Jewish

13

scholar, Saadia, began his commentary on the *Song* with these words: "Know, my brother, that you will find great differences in interpretation of the Song of Songs. In truth they differ because the Song of Songs resembles locks to which the keys have been lost."[1]

This book of the Old Testament has only eight chapters, but in proportion to its size no other book, of either the Bible or any other literature, has been given such scholarly attention, especially to its interpretation.[2] Basically, biblical exegetes down through the centuries have lined themselves up into two main camps: those holding out for the literal interpretation and those holding to the allegorical meaning. Through much intensive work in this past century in the ancient languages of the Near and Middle East and through archaeological studies, the literal school has tended to divide into varieties of the naturalistic interpretation, which treats the *Song* simply and literally as a poem about human love, or as a combination of traditional love lyrics from Egypt, Syria and other ancient countries of the Near and Middle East. In the 19th century more pedantic scholars proposed that it was written as a drama of five acts with the main actors as the Shepherd, the Shepherdess and King Solomon. Other scholars came forth with the fertility rite theory that saw vestiges of the *Song* taken from the popular fertility cults of a certain geographical area of the East. Finally, in the literal school, it was proposed to have been an epithalamium or wedding poem composed for a royal wedding.

The allegorists divide into many schools. The Jew predominately saw the *Song* as an allegory of the love of Yahweh for his people Israel or for the Torah. Among Christian allegorists, Hippolytus and Origen were two of the earliest exegetes who not only saw it as an allegory of Christ espousing himself to his bride, the church, but also of Christ as the bridegroom of the bride, the individual Christian. One commentator who did most through his sermons on the *Song* to develop the mysticism of Christ and the individual Christian was St. Bernard in the 12th century. In his 86 sermons he only arrived at the end of the second chapter! Also in the 12th century Rupert, Abbot of Deutz, wrote a commentary on the *Song* with the Blessed Virgin as the bride of Christ.

This started a whole movement both in commentaries on the *Song* and in spiritual writings of allegorizing the bride as the Virgin Mary.

Typology

The danger of such allegorizing of the *Song* is that soon there were produced strange and very artificial ways of interpreting this beautiful book of the Bible. These allegorizations moved farther and farther from any literal meaning until they sounded like sheer fantasies with no sense of objectivity or grounding in God's revelation. But can there not be another type of presentation of the *Song*? In the history of biblical exegesis we find, both in the Alexandrian as well as the Antiochian Schools of exegesis, a type of interpretation called typology.

Typological exegesis works along very different lines than does sheer allegory. It is a technique for highlighting the relationships between the two Testaments. It does not denigrate or ignore the literal interpretation in the mind of the original author(s), but it builds upon this and goes beyond. Its basic principle is the belief that the events and personages of the Old Testament were 'types" of, i.e., they prefigured and anticipated, the events and personages of the New Testament. Such an approach is rooted in the history of salvation and sees it as the scene of the progressive unfolding of God's consistent redemptive purpose.

Origen theoretically distinguished three levels of meaning in scripture corresponding to the three parts of human nature: the corporal, the psychic, and the spiritual. The first was the evident, historical sense. The second was the moral meaning or lesson of the text for the will of the individual pondering scripture prayerfully. The third was the mystical sense in relation to Christ, the church, or the great truths of the faith. But, in practice, especially in his interpretation of the *Song*, Origen used levels of interpretation that considered 1) the plain, literal sense, 2) the typological sense centered on the primacy of Christ behind all scripture, and 3) the spiritual sense in which the text was applied to the devout soul, especially in relationship to Christ.

A Parable About God's Love

I have presented the above history of biblical exegesis in order to describe more accurately what I wanted to do in writing this book. I have found inspiration for an approach to the *Song* that avoids the pitfalls of either a strict allegorical or a literal interpretation in the work of Cardinal Augustin Bea on the *Song*, along with the type of mystical writing of St. Gregory of Nyssa in his *Life of Moses*.

In his commentary on the *Song* the outstanding biblical scholar Cardinal Bea suggests that there is one literal sense, the metaphorical, in which the canticle as a whole treats only of the higher union of God and his people. He stresses that the *Song* should be seen more as a *parable* and not an allegory in which each detail has a higher meaning.[3] Bea insists that none of the individual units within the love poem has any significance independent of the general theme of mutual love. He sees with Origen that the direct inspirer of this work, the Holy Spirit, had as part of the literal meaning the unfolding of Yahweh's infinite and perfect love for his people shown in its fullest sense in Christ in his love for his church. The *Song* is messianic in its fullest meaning.

St. Gregory of Nyssa uses a similar typological approach in his classic on the spiritual life, *The Life of Moses*. St. Gregory uses the biblical account of Moses, not as a historical biography, but as a *parable* of the Christian spiritual ascent, the story of you and me in our meeting with God "in the cloud" of unknowing. Revelation is the grounding for St. Gregory's teachings on the spiritual life, of how through the spiritual senses we can perceive God who is totally invisible and incomprehensible to the created mind through baptismal and ascetical purification, by effort and virtues. Man can perceive God, through communion in Christ and the Holy Spirit, the one who is beyond all creation and visible representation.[4]

I do not intend in this book to present another biblical commentary on the *Song of Songs*. I ground myself on the great truth about God's passionate desire to communicate himself in continuous communion of a highly mystical oneness as revealed throughout scripture, and on the constant teaching of the church. I wish to present here a teaching about the mystical union brought about through ascetical practices of purifications and the development of Christ-like virtues. I presuppose always from scripture and church teaching that God's uncreated, personalized energies of love are always surrounding us to bring us into this transformative union.

Jesus taught his great truths through parables. The details and logical coherence of such parables were not primary in his intent. The listeners or readers were to take such stories to prayer. His Spirit would unfold in each parable another facet of truth that would lead them to embrace him who is "the Way, the Truth and the Life" (Jn 14:6).

Such an approach is disconcerting to a logical mind-set. This book has been written for those who have already begun to live in that affective union with Christ, their beloved, because they have determined by God's grace to do all to purify their hearts so that they may "see" God dwelling within them. Through such interior struggles to leave all in order to find all, they already know experientially that they are mystically united to Christ and nothing can separate them from him as long as they walk in humility. They will understand that my aim for this book, using the parable of the *Song of Songs*, is to show that Christ's love is stronger than death!

I present this as a book to be prayed out. Meditations and considerations are not neatly ordered. Yet this is a book to aid persons already accustomed to a more contemplative style of prayer to pray out the biblical *Song of Songs*. It is a book about God's great love for you.

Such a love is "Yahweh's flame" (Sg 8:6). It is a flash of fire which transforms the purified Christian into a love that burns constantly to be in loving union with the entire world through loving service. Could I be so bold as to suggest that this book be read and prayed in the spirit that prompted St. Bernard to write his *Sermons* on the *Song of Songs*?

> In this Marriage-Song it is the holy love behind the
> words that has to be considered, more than the words

themselves. For love speaks in it everywhere; if anyone would understand the things he reads in it, then let him love! For he who does not love will hear and read the *Song* in vain; the cold heart cannot grasp its burning eloquence. It is with Love as with a language, such as Greek or Latin: just as, unless you know the tongue yourself you will not understand it when you hear it spoken, so to the man who does not love Love's language appears crude, and will be only sounding brass and tinkling cymbals in his ears.[5]

GEORGE A. MALONEY, S.J.

Prologue

(1: 2-4)

The Bride:

> Let him kiss me with the kisses of his mouth.
> Your love is more delightful than wine;
> delicate is the fragrance of your perfume,
> your name is an oil poured out,
> and that is why the maidens love you.
> Draw me in your footsteps, let us run.
> The King has brought me into his rooms;
> you will be our joy and our gladness.
> We shall praise your love above wine;
> how right it is to love you.

Ardent Longings of the Bride for the Bridegroom

Let him kiss me with the kisses of his mouth (v. 2).

1. Love is never a linear journey from one point to another. It is rather a circular movement that increases the union of two persons. It contains all other previous moments of absence and presence, of hungering and of being fed by mutual giving and receiving, still the present moment of desire is new, never before experienced in the same intensity and longing for union with the beloved. And tomorrow will bring new desires and new pains to prepare for a new loving union.

This is the way the *Song of Songs* begins. The bride, almost in a wild frenzy, cries out her longing for her spouse to kiss her with the kisses of his mouth. This is the Christian, you and I, called by God's free choice in his son, Jesus Christ, through his Holy Spirit, to enter into the deepest union with the indwelling Trinity.

Your burning desire comes first before the union is attained. Yet you can be certain, with the knowledge of the Holy Spirit, that God so wishes you to desire ardently for such a union. That is why God has created you—to become one with Christ and share in his oneness with the heavenly Father.

It is not ecstatic feelings you long for. It is the total fulfillment of the desires God's Spirit has placed deep within the fibers of your being. Your plea for the kisses of Christ, your spouse, is God's own desire which he constantly expresses in you through his Spirit. God gives you the power to utter such a seemingly naive prayer. This union of all unions with the God-man, Jesus Christ, is the very prayer he utters continually from within you. Do you think it is your own burning desire for this union with Christ? You humbly utter it, because God wishes to grant what you ask for much more than you could ever desire it. You love him because he first loved you (1 Jn 4:19).

This is Christ's prayer that begins to be fulfilled in you by your ardent desire for the greatest union possible with God:

> Father, may they be one in us,
> as you are in me and I am in you,
> so that the world may believe it was you who sent me.
> I have given them the glory you gave to me,
> that they may be one as we are one.
> With me in them and you in me,
> may they be so completely one
> that the world will realize that it was you who sent me
> and that I have loved them as much as you loved me
> (Jn 17:21-23).

It is sharing in Moses' prayer to Yahweh: "Show me your glory, I beg you" (Ex 33:18). It is the longing of all contemplative Christians who want more of God's presence, as St. John of the Cross so beautifully expresses the bride's plea in *The Spiritual Canticle:*

> Reveal Your presence,
> And may the vision of Your beauty be my death;
> For the sickness of love
> is not cured
> Except by Your very presence and image (Stanza 11).[1]

20

The Kiss Is the Holy Spirit

2. It is St. Bernard in his commentary on the *Song of Songs* who teaches that the kisses from the mouth of Christ, the spouse of the Christian bride, are no less than the Holy Spirit.[2]

The Father is the mind who expresses his love for his children through Jesus Christ, his mouth. Christ kisses us with the kisses of his mouth by giving us the Holy Spirit who makes possible this most intimate union between us individually and Christ. St. Bernard describes this ineffable mystery:

> But it was the kiss of the kiss, not of the mouth. Listen if you will know what the kiss of the mouth is: "The Father and I are one;" and again: "I am in the Father and the Father is in me." This is a kiss from mouth to mouth, beyond the claim of any creature. It is a kiss of love and of peace, but of the love which is beyond all knowledge, and that peace which is so much greater than we can understand. The truth is that the things that no eye has seen and no ear has heard, things beyond the mind of man, were revealed to Paul by God through his Spirit, that is, through him who is the kiss of his mouth. That the Son is in the Father and the Father in the Son signifies the kiss of the mouth. But the kiss of the kiss we discover when we read: "Instead of the spirit of the world, we have received the Spirit that comes from God," to teach us to understand the gifts that he has given us.[3]

This is what it truly means to be charismatic: to be fervently desirous to receive the kisses, the gifts of the Holy Spirit, so that the individual Christian may enter into the transforming union through love with the Holy Trinity. For the bride knows by faith in God's revealed truth through the word made flesh, Jesus Christ, that it is the work of the Holy Spirit to divinize her into Christ's beloved. It is the Spirit who makes you one with Christ, so you live no longer you yourself but Christ lives in you (Gal 2:20). "These are the very things that God has revealed to us through the Spirit, for the Spirit reaches the depths of everything, even the depths of God...we have received the Spirit that comes from God, to teach us to understand the gifts that he has given us...it can only be understood by means of the Spirit" (1 Cor 2:10,12,14).

St. Augustine learned through the Spirit to experience God's most intimate presence as that of God dwelling within the Christian: "I did not find you without, Lord, because I wrongly sought you without, who were within."[4] Only the Spirit of the Father and the Son can reveal to you that they dwell within you (Jn 14:23). Their love for you, which will transform you into Christ's most beautiful bride and give you the strength to bear all sufferings in order to come into this union for all eternity, can be experienced by you only through the Holy Spirit (Rom 5:5).

3. You ask for the kisses of Christ's mouth only when you have prepared yourself properly by your kisses, first to the feet of Christ and then his hand, as St. Bernard describes the purgative and illuminative paths preceding the unitive way.[5]

First you are to cast yourself at Christ's feet as the sinful woman did to weep for sins and receive his forgiving love. Then Christ lifts you up, strengthens you in your weakness to run in his ways of virtues. Then with fear and trembling, yet with assurance of Christ himself, that if you ask, you will receive (Lk 11:9), you can ask for the kisses of his mouth, the most intimate oneness with him.

The Beauty of the Spouse

> Your love is more delightful than wine;
> delicate is the fragrance of your perfume,
> your name is an oil poured out,
> and that is why the maidens love you.
> Draw me in your footsteps, let us run (v. 2-4).

The bride begins to praise her spouse for his love[6] to her. The symbols used are of creatures that appeal powerfully to the physical sense, which attract by an intoxication, a soothing refreshment, bringing joy, contentment and well-being.

1. The Christian, who has tasted and seen how sweet the Lord is (Ps 34:8), becomes intoxicated with his beauty. Wine in the East is a symbol of joy, refreshment, rest and pleasure. "Wine to make

them cheerful," says the psalmist (Ps 104:15). It is the Holy Spirit who pours new wine into the heart of the contemplative who is ready to stretch to possess Christ at the cost of any other attachments or false securities (Lk 5:37-38).

Christ's love is to be preferred by you over all other loves. For you have already experienced what joy his indwelling presence brings you that makes all other created joys pale. Christ is your beloved, your lover and comforter. He is constant and unchanging in his love for you. "Jesus Christ is the same today as he was yesterday and as he will be for ever" (Heb 13:8). Of him Jeremiah spoke: "I have loved you with an everlasting love, so I am constant in my affection for you" (Jer 31:3).

2. Tender and delicate is Christ's love for you as a subtle fragrance of perfume. Such a human-divine love of Christ for you permeates you gently and again fills you with an inner intoxication of uplifting beauty. Perfume oil was highly regarded in the Near East and used by both men and women (2 Kgs 20:13) as a sign of wealth. Such perfume oil, when used, diffused its delightful fragrance to all the bystanders. Christ's love for you is to be absorbed into all parts of your being, allowing you to spread the fragrance of his love to all you meet.

3. The name of Jesus in Semitic usage stands for the essence of him as God who saves or heals. It is a healing oil poured out to soothe all the weary who call on his name and his loving presence.

> But God raised him high
> and gave him the name
> which is above all other names
> so that all beings
> in the heavens, on earth and in the underworld,
> should bend the knee at the name of Jesus
> and that every tongue should acclaim
> Jesus Christ as Lord,
> to the glory of God the Father (Phil 2:9-11).

How sweet and healing it is for you in all your trials to call often on the name of Jesus and to discover his living presence within you. This is the only name and presence on the face of the earth

23

whereby you can be healed of your fears (Acts 4: 12) for his perfect love casts away all your fears (1 Jn 4:18). In his name and presence you will ask anything of the Father and he will give it to you (Jn 16:23-26).

Unceasing prayer becomes possible when the name and presence of Jesus enter into your *heart*, the deepest consciousness and core of your being where you meet him in the constant embrace of bride and groom, made one through the Spirit. His presence continues even during your sleep, becoming a source of constant peace and joy. This prayer as a state of permanent and yet ever-increasing consciousness comes from the Spirit of Jesus who makes this level of awareness possible through his infusion of faith, hope and love into your heart. Such loving awareness is like an oil poured out to comfort you in your struggles to stand inwardly attentive, to bring every mood, thought and feeling under his dominance (2 Cor 10:5).

4. "And that is why the maidens love you." Who are the "maidens" who love Christ? The bride praises her spouse and implies that there are many others who wish to follow him as she does. They love Christ, as she does, for who he is and for his perfect beauty, which captivates all who open up to receive his love.

Their love is a strong, "feeling" love, drawn to Christ by his nearness and human attractiveness. Thus "maidens" could stand for those Christians who are still in the first fervor of being attracted to a greater union with Christ, as many of the early Fathers interpreted this word.[7] It would also include those, like the bride, who have already advanced in a deep love for Christ. In whichever group you place yourself, know that greater trials and purifications await you to test your response of love for Christ. Know that the delights of Christ must yield in your desire to be one in him, to love him as he loves you. "In your minds you must be the same as Christ Jesus:...he emptied himself to assume the condition of a slave...he was humbler yet, even to accepting death, death on a cross" (Phil 2:5-8).

5. "Draw me...." The bride of Christ humbly begs that he be the drawing force. She is incapable of following him by her own

powers. She confesses by this statement that fervent desires for the delights of Christ are not enough to sustain her in seeking only him.

We see here the beginning of what will become a greater awareness: the poverty of one's own power—or even the consolations received in following Christ—to sustain the Christian amidst the trials that will come from being the bride of Christ.

If Christ draws you, you will run in his ways, and other persons like you will be drawn by your example and prayerfulness to run with you toward greater oneness with Christ.

Unless Christ himself draws us, we will be unable to follow him. And he draws us to himself through the revelation of the Holy Spirit who makes us aware of Christ's infinite love for us, especially on the cross. "And when I am lifted up from the earth, I shall draw all men to myself" (Jn 12:32). Jesus teaches you clearly in the gospels that he is "the Way, the Truth and the Life" (Jn 14:6) who leads us to the Father.

> "No one can come to me
> unless he is drawn by the Father who sent me,
> and I will raise him up at the last day"
> (Jn 6:44).

Without Me You Can Do Nothing

The Prologue ends with the humble plea of the bride that her spouse, Christ, be her strength, drawing her to ever deeper levels of loving union with him. The remaining love poems are a poetic description of what you can be assured of: that when you humbly place all your strength in Christ, as you confess your own weakness, he will be your power. St. Paul experienced this through his journey of faith as the Lord assured him:

> But he (Christ) has said, "My grace is enough for you: my power is at its best in weakness." So I shall be very happy to make my weaknesses my special boast so that the power of Christ may stay over me, and that is why I am quite content with my weaknesses, and with insults, hardships, persecutions, and the agonies I go through for Christ's sake. For it is when I am weak that I am strong (2 Cor 12:9-10).

25

You can be sure that Jesus is always answering your ardent pleas that he draw you to ever greater oneness with him. He teaches you: "I tell you therefore: everything you ask and pray for, believe that you have it already, and it will be yours" (Mk 11:24).

The prologue to mystical union lays this foundation for your faith, hope and love to grow through all succeeding trials and purifications. This foundational belief is that Jesus loves you already, infinitely. He will not give you his new love only because you ask for it. Your petition, when sincerely and humbly offered to him through his love poured into your heart through his Holy Spirit (Rom 5:5), is answered when you surrender to his perfect love for you that is always present.

He will always be there, loving you with the madness of his love for you on the cross. He will meet all your needs, not giving anything new once he eternally has given you all things in the gift of his spousal love for you. It is you who need in your life to believe you already have his infinite love drawing you, so you and others can run freely and generously after him only to discover he has always been within you.

> I myself taught Ephraim to walk,
> I took them in my arms;
> yet they have not understood that I was the one
> looking after them.
> I led them with reins of kindness,
> with leading-strings of love (Hos 11:3-4).

The Inner Mansions of the King

> The King has brought me into his rooms;
> you will be our joy and our gladness.
> We shall praise your love above wine;
> how right it is to love you (v. 4).

1.   The Prologue ends with the king appearing and drawing the beloved into his inner rooms. The accent is on an interior chamber, hidden from other rooms to secure privacy, intimacy and loving union. All you need do is to thirst for the living waters

of Christ's Holy Spirit (Jn 7:37-38, Is 55:1) and he will lead you into his interior chamber where he will love you most ardently, enrapturing you and transforming you by his love into his very own bride.

But the good news Jesus came to reveal to us and make possible is that this interior chamber is none other than what scripture calls the *heart*. Christ asks you to give him your heart (Prv 23:26 NAB). It is into your heart, the inner closet (Mt 6:6), that you are to enter and there surrender yourself to Christ, your Lord and king, who has won your heart or has gained entrance into your affections by dying for you.

Your heart, the innermost core of your being, where you discover your true self in the oneness with Christ, is to be the "place" where Christ the King leads you. He inebriates you by the beauty of his divine-human person. Here in your heart he meets you in an *I-Thou* relationship. He, the king of the world, has died for you. That love for you hurled him into a new, resurrectional life which he now at each moment wishes to share with you.

2.   You enter into this intimacy alone with Christ. But you now recognize your oneness with him as a joy and gladness, which you share with others. He is your king, your spouse, but he is also *your* joy and gladness. You share that overflowing ecstasy with others who experience their unique, personal oneness with Christ. Yet they, too, know that you and others share with them a similar oneness under the same head, Christ, the king and spouse of all who mystically are united with him.

3.   That is why you can joyfully speak to your king, Jesus Christ, and say: "We shall praise your love above wine." In your oneness you can never be truly enraptured beyond any intoxication or gladness that wine can bring to your heart without singing praises with others in the body of Christ for what the king of all does for one and all, for one member in his body and for all members in the same body. "If one part is given special honor, all parts enjoy it" (1 Cor 12:26).

4.   Yes, overwhelmed by Christ's perfect, self-emptying love for you, you constantly, with great reverence and humility, utter from the depths of your being: "How right it is to love you!"

27

First Poem

(1:5-2:7)

The Bride Speaks to Her Spouse

> I am black but lovely, daughters of Jerusalem,
> like the tents of Kedar,
> like the pavilions of Salmah.
> Take no notice of my swarthiness,
> it is the sun that has burnt me.
>
> My mother's sons turned their anger on me,
> they made me look after the vineyards.
> Had I only looked after my own!
>
> Tell me then, you whom my heart loves:
> Where will you lead your flock to graze,
> where will you rest it at noon?
> That I may no more wander like a vagabond
> beside the flocks of your companions (1:5-7).

1 "I am black but lovely...." The bride, after she has been led by the king into his inner chamber, confronts the daughters of Jerusalem, who chide her out of jealousy that she, who is "black," has pretended to be the equal of the king. Origen interprets these daughters on one level as of the earthly Jerusalem, the Jewish people, who, "seeing the church of the Gentiles, despise and vilify her for her ignoble birth...."[8]

In a mystical interpretation, the bride stands for the fervent Christian who, in spite of past sins and present failings, knows she has become beautiful through the workings of Jesus' Spirit. The daughters represent the Christians who follow Christ but are lukewarm and ready to criticize others more fervent.

29

One of the signs of a Christian being led by Christ into a deeper, contemplative prayer is a sense of humility and truth. The Spirit of Jesus leads such a person of prayer away from the first flush of feeling prayer, which so often inflates one with a spiritual pride, to encounter Christ by deeper faith, but also by a realization of his or her own sinfulness.

The working of God's grace to instill into the serious Christian an anxiety, fear and disgust as he or she confronts existence in the light of the "not-yet," or inauthentic "non-being," is not merely a reflection on death and a cry for immortality. It is an ontological "nostalgia" to leave the "husks of swine," to leave one's sinful nature, symbolized by darkness, and return to one's true self, where one lives in the light of God in whom there is no darkness or sinfulness.

Here the bride shows the delicate balance between what she is without Christ and yet what she is now through his loving grace. The deeper you go into your unconscious being, the more you will discover the sin and death that have not yet been conquered by the new life Christ comes to give you.

St. John of the Cross in *The Spiritual Canticle*, a loose commentary on the *Song of Songs*, gives us his rendition of this verse:

> Do not despise me;
> For if, before, You found me dark,
> Now truly You can look at me
> Since You have looked
> And left in me grace and beauty.[9]

But Lovely

2. By confronting the false ego, the contemplative brings the perfect love of God, as experienced in the indwelling presence of Christ, to heal the fears that drive the soul into the dark world of unreality: "In love there can be no fear, but fear is driven out by perfect love" (1 Jn 4:18). As the darkness of your sinful nature lifts before the transfiguring light of the indwelling Christ, you begin to see that you also radiate a new beauty—a sharing in Christ's beauty.

You realize paradoxically that you are lovely, worthy to be loved, as you actually are, by God, the Trinity, and capable of loving others freely; yet all this beauty is sheer gift from God. You participate in God's very own nature (2 Pt 1:4). Christ's love, poured into your heart through His Spirit, lifts you up to see yourself as not only loved infinitely by Christ, but as beautiful and desirable to him.

Praise is constantly on your lips and in your heart as you humbly rejoice in what God in his greatness and humility has done to bring about your transformation from dark to light, from a sinful nature in Adam to a new creation in Christ (2 Cor 5:17).

You share in Mary's joy as her exultation becomes yours:

> My soul proclaims the greatness of the Lord
> and my spirit exults in God my savior;
> because he has looked upon his lowly handmaid.
> Yes, from this day forward all generations
>   will call me blessed,
> for the Almighty has done great things for me.
> Holy is his name,
> and his mercy reaches from age to age for those
>   who fear him (Lk 1:46-50).

3.   The bride uses a powerful comparison to describe the coexistence of her sinful, false self and her beautiful, true self. She is like the "tents of Kedar." Psalm 120:5 describes life in Kedar as a living in hell: "This is worse than a life in Mesheck, or camping in Kedar!" These were the tents of the second son of Ishmael (Gn 25:13). No people were more despised by the Jews than such "barbarians." Jews would not come near such tents, usually made of black goatskins.

Thus the bride is telling the daughters of Jerusalem that exteriorly she is not beautiful. But then she claims her inner beauty by speaking of the pavilions of Salmah or Solomon. For the Jewish mind such inner sanctuary, separated by beautiful, white curtains, is the picture of enlightenment and perfection. Outwardly she may appear dark and even despicable. But by God's mercy, manifested to her by the indwelling beautiful Christ through his perfect love for her, she is radiantly beautiful. Born of God, she no longer sins because God's seed is within her (1 Jn 3:9), lifting her up to be Christ's long-desired bride.

4. She begs humbly that her listeners not judge her by her dark appearance (v. 6). She seeks to explain how she became swarthy in color. It was the sun that scorched her. This is an image of a person living on a purely natural level, living in the natural light that gradually renders her unattractive.

We have been born into such a light that only produces darkness. With King David we can confess: "You know I was born guilty, a sinner from the moment of conception" (Ps 51:5). Yet, as a Christian, you cannot forget that Christ has transformed your sinfulness into a new life in him.

> If it is certain that death reigned over everyone as the consequence of one man's fall, it is even more certain that one man, Jesus Christ, will cause everyone to reign in life who receives the free gift that he does not deserve, of being made righteous (Rom 5:17).

You need not live the life you formerly led. The blood of Jesus, God's Son, "purifies us from all sin" (1 Jn 1:7).

Neglect of One's Inner Life

5. Many meanings can be found in the bride's reasons for her appearance. Perhaps St. Bernard's application to contemplatives may apply to you. He writes:

> Taking vineyards to mean souls, I often reproach myself for having taken on the care of other souls without being even capable of caring for my own....Certainly those who put me to looking after vineyards must have fully realized how badly I kept my own. But, alas! How long did I keep it uncultivated and deserted...? How many and how wonderful were the clusters of good works contaminated by my anger, stolen from me by pride, or spoiled and ruined by conceit?...This was the condition it was in and yet they made me look after the vineyards without considering what needed to be done to mine or what had been done, heedless of the apostle's words (1 Tm 3,5): How can any man who does not understand how to manage his own family have responsibility for the church of God?[10]

How often in the past have you concerned yourself with working "in the vineyards" of others, including your own family and relatives, while neglecting first to discover your true self within the vineyard of your own heart? Can you truly serve others lovingly if you do not love yourself in Christ? Can you visit your brother or sister in prison before you have ministered to yourself, locked behind bars you created? How can you feed the hungry and give the thirsty to drink before you have had a proper respect and love for yourself?

Search for the True Shepherd

6.   The bride turns back to speak to her beloved. She craves greater intimacy with him. She wishes to belong to his flock, be his sheep, to graze under his loving care and protection. She wishes to be near him to take her rest at noon, the sign of perfection and total completion.[11] She is weary of wandering about like a vagabond, following other flocks, but not that of her beloved.

You have undoubtedly felt in your following of Christ his call, given by the Holy Spirit, to enter into a deeper, more intimate relationship with Christ "whom your heart loves." You craved to be fed by your Good Shepherd not only with his teaching but with a constant feeding on him dwelling within you. You were tired of wandering about in the hot desert. You wanted to rest near waters of repose, to enter into high noon, a completion or fulfillment of your potentialities locked within you to know and love your shepherd, Christ. Remember the first time Psalm 23 gripped and filled you with burning desire to surrender yourself more completely to him?

> Yahweh is my shepherd,
>   I lack nothing.
> In meadows of green grass he lets me lie.
> To the waters of repose he leads me;
>   there he revives my soul.
>
> He guides me by paths of virtue
>   for the sake of his name.
>
> Though I pass through a gloomy valley,
>   I fear no harm;

> beside me your rod and your staff
>   are there, to hearten me.
>
> You prepare a table before me
>   under the eyes of my enemies;
> you anoint my head with oil,
>   my cup brims over.
>
> Ah, how goodness and kindness pursue me,
>   every day of my life;
> my home, the house of Yahweh,
>   as long as I live (Ps 23).

The good news is that, when you truly love Christ and ardently desire to be more totally his, you discover he is already dwelling most intimately within you with the Father and Holy Spirit. You pray to discover where your beloved dwells. You wish to leave your wanderings, where you followed other teachers, to follow Christ completely. The prayer is answered, not by Christ coming to you, but by you, through his Spirit, discovering him waiting at the door of your heart (Rv 3:20) for you to surrender.

It is not outside you will find your Good Shepherd, but it is within that you are to find him who always has been there. Why have you not found him earlier? You needed to wander about, before you could realize that only Christ can satisfy all the love yearnings within your heart.

The Chorus to the Bride

> If you do not know this, O loveliest of women,
> follow the tracks of the flock,
> and take your kids to graze
> close by the shepherds' tents (1:8).

1.   It is disputed among commentators and translators whether these lines are spoken by the spouse (Christ) or by a chorus of the daughters of Jerusalem. For our purposes, whether it is Christ speaking directly to his bride or a chorus addressing the bride of Christ and giving the teaching of Christ, the text contains an instruction for the bride. If she has not yet attained the deepest union

with her spouse, she is exhorted to follow the example of the majority of the flock (the sheep who wish to follow Christ, the shepherd). She is encouraged to use her senses, develop her emotions and imagination through discursive, mental prayer. She is to stay close to the teachings of the shepherds, those given authority by Christ in the church to teach the sheep safe doctrine applicable to all.

Part of following the voices of the shepherds is to strive to acquire the basic virtues necessary to advance to higher levels of perfection. There a greater intimacy with the groom will await the bride. But until such union has been attained, the bride is to stay close in obedience to legitimate teachers who give safe norms to be followed by all who have not yet entered into a bridal union with their Lord.

2. We could also read this text as a chiding from the chorus, or from Christ himself. If the bride has already tasted intimacy with Christ, her spouse, and yet still refuses to understand how she is to live in complete abandonment to him, then she should follow the way of beginners in the spiritual life.

Attachments to Consolations

Such is the story of many who have entered into a deeper contemplative prayer life. They still do not understand what Christ is doing in their lives. They seek, not Christ, but more and more delights and consolations. They lack the courage to surrender every desire for self-satisfaction to Christ to seek total happiness in complete surrender to him.

Such Christians reach the beginning of the spiritual desert. But the call to find security in sense pleasures and consolations rather than in blind faith and obedience to the indwelling spouse is too strong. They return to the fleshpots of Egypt rather than go deeper into the wilds of the untamed false ego within themselves. Yielding to their desires for sense pleasures turns them away from their union with Christ. But now the bondage becomes greater because of a spirit of self-righteousness that develops. They rationalize themselves into a position that insists that God thinks as they do. Added to this is a hidden, gnawing guilt that they have really turned away from God. Caught in the vice of self-absorption, such Christians find repentance extremely difficult.

The author of the Book of Hebrews is very condemning of such backsliding Christians:

> As for those people who were once brought into the light, and tasted the gift from heaven, and received a share of the Holy Spirit, and appreciated the good message of God and the powers of the world to come and yet in spite of this have fallen away—it is impossible for them to be renewed a second time. They cannot be repentant if they have willfully crucified the Son of God and openly mocked him. A field that has been well watered by frequent rain, and gives the crops that are wanted by the owners who grew them, is given God's blessing; but one that grows brambles and thistles is abandoned, and practically cursed. It will end by being burnt (Heb 6:4-8).

Praise From the Bridegroom

The Bridegroom Speaks

> To my mare harnessed to Pharaoh's chariot
> I compare you, my love.
> Your cheeks show fair between their pendants
> and your neck within its necklaces.
> We shall make you golden earrings
> and beads of silver (1:9-11).

1.   The spouse now addresses his bride and compares her to his mare harnessed to Pharaoh's chariot. He addresses her tenderly as his love. He is pleased with her efforts to follow him and run after him with burning desires, but also with effective strength and power. Christ singles out his chosen bride and describes by comparisons the inner beauty that draws him so lovingly toward her.

In the time of Solomon the best horses came from Egypt (cf. 1 Kgs 10:28-29). The bride was born in Egypt in the bondage of Pharaoh. Yet she possesses God-given natural talents. Her first external beauty is compared to the finest of horses, highly spirited with fiery energy and power. She possesses speed that symbolizes spiritual swiftness in following him if she continues to "pass-over" out of self-centered bondage into the freedom of his love. Christ is compared to King Solomon who goes down to Pharaoh and buys this finest of horses and takes her for his own. What a cost he paid for her in his own blood!

2. The bride is praised for her cheeks that stand out as fair in complexion between the earrings that hang from the ears and set off her beautiful face. Her neck is beautified by its necklaces. The spouse praises his bride's natural beauty, for a woman is considered beautiful in her face and neck. Yet he adds other elements to her natural endowments, as the earrings and necklaces, as if to show that one needs to highlight natural gifts by the adornment of supernatural gifts of graces and virtues.

Work of the Holy Spirit

3. The spouse changes from *I* to *We* as he promises to make for his bride other earrings of gold and beaded necklaces of silver. In the mystical union between Christ and the Christian soul, his bride, who can the we be? Christ is pleased with the bride's natural beauty and her cooperation in developing the adorning beauty of virtues and graces. But he promises her that he and his Holy Spirit will personally be involved in making for her earrings of gold and beads of silver.

The divine goldsmiths are freely to fashion for her adornments that will enhance her beauty. St. Paul said that we see now only faintly what we will in heaven see face to face: "The knowledge that I have now is imperfect; but then I shall know as fully as I am known" (1 Cor 13:12). It is the work of the Holy Spirit to pierce our inner ears with the gold of divinity so that we can even now know as God knows by possessing a share in his wisdom.

Jesus releases the power of his Spirit, who divinizes us through his divine gifts of knowledge, understanding and wisdom. We know by the Spirit's enlightenment how passionately we are loved by God in Jesus Christ. We can know how beautiful we have been made by the Spirit's transforming love. We can believe

37

that Christ ardently loves us as his own bride by the deifying power of the Spirit.

The beads wrought out of silver can refer to the humanity of Jesus who through his humanity redeems us. It is again his work with the Holy Spirit that brings about the Christian's true transformation, making known God's love for the bride through his sacrifice unto the last drop of blood. That living love is recognized as abiding within the Christian and always beautifying the bride as she surrenders in complete obedience to her spouse.

Dialogue Between the Bride and the Bridegroom

—While the King rests in his own room
my nard yields its perfume.
My Beloved is a sachet of myrrh
lying between my breasts.
My Beloved is a cluster of henna flowers
among the vines of Engedi.

—How beautiful you are, my love,
how beautiful you are!
Your eyes are doves.

—How beautiful you are, my Beloved,
and how delightful!
All green is our bed.

—The beams of our house are of cedar,
the panelling of cypress.

—I am the rose of Sharon,
the lily of the valleys.
—As a lily among the thistles,
so is my love among the maidens.
—As an apple tree among the trees of the orchard,
so is my Beloved among the young men.
In his longed-for shade I am seated
and his fruit is sweet to my taste.
He has taken me to his banquet hall,

and the banner he raises over me is love.
Feed me with raisin cakes,
restore me with apples,
for I am sick with love.

His left arm is under my head,
his right embraces me.

—I charge you,
daughters of Jerusalem,
by the gazelles, by the hinds of the field,
not to stir my love, nor rouse it,
until it please to awake (1:12—2:7).

1.   The two lovers are found together in deepest intimacy. The
bride seems to be watching her beloved rest in his room on his
couch and is thinking aloud. The Son rests in perfect oneness with
the heavenly Father. And the bride has been led by her spouse
into this inner sanctum where he is the one "nearest to the Father's
heart" (Jn 1:18). She considers humbly her lowliness and yet is
overcome with what her lover has done for her. She is being
brought into a similar "resting," not only with Christ, but, one
with Christ, she is to share also a oneness with the heavenly Father
and the Spirit.

2.   She says that her nard suffuses its perfume in his room. Nard
is an aromatic oil extracted from a plant that grows in northern
and eastern India.[14] What the bride contrasts is her lowliness (as
the nard plant is quite insignificant in size and appearance) with
her beauty brought about by the spouse's love for her. It is her
humble realization of what she is without her spouse contrasted
in laudatory terms with what she is through his gift of love.

Mary, the mother of Jesus, has always stood as the archetype
of the Christian contemplative, as she sang in her inner poverty
the glories of what her Lord had done to her: "My soul proclaims
the greatness of the Lord and my spirit exults in God my savior;
because he has looked upon his lowly handmaid" (Lk 1:46-47).

Need of Humility

The bridegroom, Christ, reveals himself to you to the degree that you are rooted in humility and in love. When you keep ever in mind your nothingness, along with what Christ has mercifully done to admit you into the intimacy of his oneness with the Father through the Spirit of love, you will also experience the perfume of ecstatic praise and constant wonderment.

3.   In the gospels Mary, the sister of Martha and Lazarus, poured out a costly nard ointment that symbolized both her complete devotion to Christ and the anointing of Christ for his death and burial (Jn 12:3, Mk 14:3; Mt 26:6-13). Here is accentuated the costliness of the nard, which is poured out and fills the entire house with its perfume. Such a perfume brings a great price. To anoint Christ as your king will demand from you a constant sacrifice of everything in order that you can become a precious perfume to him.

Bittersweet Myrrh

4.   The bride likens her beloved to a sachet of myrrh which lies between her breasts. Refined ladies of the East, by way of perfuming themselves, carried thus a small sachet of myrrh to continually give off a pervading fragrance. Here the bride first refers to her spouse as a loving presence which she carries in her breasts or heart, the scriptural reference to the seat of affections and loving union. It is the first of many times that she calls her spouse her beloved. For the Christian contemplative faith assures the bride that Christ truly lives within her heart. She carries him about throughout the day and night. He releases from within her consciousness a heavenly fragrance that others can perceive and be drawn to her, the carrier of Christ.

5.   But the element of myrrh for the Christian adds another element. For myrrh to give off its perfume, it must be bruised and crushed, as the Suffering Servant of Yahweh, Jesus Christ, would have to be bruised for our sins (Is 53:5). The Magi brought myrrh to the Christ-child at Bethlehem when God humbled himself to become a babe (Mt 2:11). The soldiers offered Jesus on the cross wine mixed with myrrh (Mk 15:23). In his death his followers wrapped him in a mixture of myrrh and aloes (Jn 19:39). Myrrh, therefore, highlights the bitterness of the sufferings Jesus accepted in his passion and humiliating death on the cross (Ph 2:7-8).

The bride of Christ knows that there can be no nuptial union with him except through the myrrh of bearing sufferings and humiliations in order to enter into a sharing in his glory. St. Paul understood this necessity of being co-crucified with Christ (Gal 2:20) in order to enter into a oneness with him. "As scripture promised: For your sake we are being massacred daily, and reckoned as sheep for the slaughter. These are the trials through which we triumph, by the power of him who loved us" (Rom 8:36-37).

St. Peter preaches to the early converts to Christianity this fundamental lesson:

> If you can have some share in the sufferings of Christ, be glad, because you will enjoy a much greater gladness when his glory is revealed. It is a blessing for you when they insult you for bearing the name of Christ, because it means that you have the Spirit of glory, the Spirit of God resting on you...but if anyone of you should suffer for being a Christian, then he is not to be ashamed of it; he should thank God that he has been called one (1 Pt 4:13-16).

A Suffering Spouse

Scripture confirms that Christ is a suffering spouse. "Truly, you are a bridegroom of blood to me" (Ex 4:25). Jesus has suffered the bitterness of his passion and death, and he promised that any who wanted to follow him would have to share in similar sufferings. But such Christians are to realize, even in the enduring of such sufferings, that Christ lives within them as a sweet fragrance, giving strength to bear all things for the privilege of having a share in him (Mk 8:34; Mt 10:38; 16:24; Lk 9:23; 14:27).

6. The bride likens her beloved to a cluster of henna flowers among the vines of Engedi. The cluster of henna flowers refers to the cypress shrub in the Near and Middle East that not only produces a cosmetic for dying hair and nails, but also, as in this reference, a perfume similar to that of the myrrh. This cluster grows in the rich oasis of Engedi near the western shore of the Dead Sea, which produces wine and fruit of the palm.

The beloved of the bride is therefore contrasted with a similar fragrance of beauty that is shared with those who are ready to endure all in order to possess such a beloved. The wine of Engedi indicates the intoxication of the bride in his beauty, which he is willing to share intimately with her.

The Bride's Beauty

7.   The spouse now praises his beloved as he sees the beauty in her, both in her complete devotion to him and in her readiness to bear all sufferings for the oneness she longs for even more than the union already attained. Can you and I not thrill at believing Jesus Christ says these words to us individually, "How beautiful you are, my love, how beautiful you are!" He wishes us to know how beautiful we have become, both exteriorly and interiorly, through his Spirit. From the inner transformation that is taking place within us as we surrender to his loving presence and his purification, this beauty is beginning to flow outward toward others whom we meet.

He praises you for your eyes resembling those of doves. The dove is the symbol of simplicity and fidelity. Your eyes focused completely and exclusively on Christ have a simplicity that centers all your pursuits and desires on the one, magnificent obsession of living only for your bridegroom, Jesus Christ.

8.   Now the bride responds to the praises of the beloved. She gives him praise for her beauty: "How beautiful you are, my Beloved, and how delightful!" Can we take credit for anything that comes to us as a gift from the Father of lights (Jas 1:17)? We, too, turn all praise and honor back to Christ whose love in his Spirit has begun the process of making us beautiful in word, deed and being before God and neighbor. We are nothing but emptied receptacles to be filled with God's gifts and to him we are to render honor and glory. The focus is no longer upon ourselves when he moves us to union with him. The bride is ravished more and more by the beauties in Christ.

9.   This stirs up in the bride the passionate desire for the nuptial union that Christ holds out to her. She declares that their bed where this nuptial union is to take place is all green. This bed is the inner closet, the heart of the contemplative where Christ comes to dwell and to give to the Christian bride the nuptial kiss.

The bed is already adorned with green a sign of growth of virtues as well as the life of Christ that is forever producing greater fruit within the bride.

10.   The bride likens the house of her groom and herself to the Temple in Jerusalem. The beams of the Temple as well as the palace of Solomon were made of cedars from Lebanon with panelling of cypress. She compares Christ, her spouse, to the strength of the beams of cedar that supported the Temple. He is her strength. But as she looks up, she sees panelling of cypress, the symbol of death. The bridal bed is covered with greenery, with the promise of new life that will come from the nuptial union. But there is the reminder always that new life comes from a dying process. The bride confesses that she has obtained some virtues, but these are only preparations for the great death when she passes over from herself to give herself in ecstatic union to live forever more for him alone, no longer to possess any part of her being outside of him.

11.   "I am the rose of Sharon, the lily of the valleys." Commentators vary as to whether this is spoken by the bride or the groom.[13] In spite of the fact that the majority of the Fathers of the West and some of the early Eastern Fathers tended to attribute this statement to the groom, modern commentators find it fits into the dialogue between the two lovers as best coming from the lips of the bride. The flower, rose of Sharon, should refer to an early spring flower, common to Israel, such as the crocus, daffodil or narcissus. The lily of the valley highlights the commonness of the spring flower that even today dots the countryside and would best refer to the red anemones that carpet the fields of Israel and probably were the flowers Christ referred to as the lilies of the field (Mt 6:28; Lk 12:27).

The bride exclaims that she has entered into a richness and abundance through the love of her groom. Although such spring flowers were quite ordinary, the bride is stressing the abundant richness and fertility that have come to her or will come in greater degrees through her intimate union with the groom.

12.   The groom turns to the bride and compares her to a lily among the thistles, so is his love among the maidens. The bride

of Christ that we strive to be by his election is one who stands out far above the crowd of persons who do not know him intimately. You have seen a lily or delicate flower among brambles and thorns. Its beauty is enhanced by the lack of beauty in the surrounding weeds and thistles. The maidens are those who live naturally and not according to the transforming power of Christ.

But the thistles also suggest that the groom holds out to his bride the reality that those surrounding her will offer her many trials and sufferings. But those very sufferings will bring out her purity and delicate beauty all the more. St. Paul well understood the promise of Christ to his followers that they would be persecuted for his name's sake, but they should rejoice and be exceedingly glad for greater union with him is possible. St. Paul writes to Timothy: "You are well aware, then, that anybody who tries to live in devotion to Christ is certain to be attacked; while these wicked impostors will go from bad to worse, deceiving others and deceived themselves" (2 Tm 3:12-13).

What sufferings await the bride of Christ from those closest to her as she enters into a deeper intimacy with him! Such persons seem to be threatened by what Christ is doing in the life of the fervent one who seeks only him. But in spite of such sufferings that await fervent souls desirous of giving themselves to their spouse, Christ, they are assured by him who call them his love. He will support them in all temptations and sufferings, psychological and spiritual and even physical, that may come from within or from others around them. It is his love that strengthens them in their weakness and allows them to do all things, for he alone is their strength. St. Paul expresses this truth when he writes: "So I shall be very happy to make my weaknesses my special boast so that the power of Christ may stay over me, and that is why I am quite content with my weaknesses, and with insults, hardships, persecutions, and the agonies I go through for Christ's sake. For it is when I am weak that I am strong" (2 Cor 12:9-10).

Christ the Apple Tree

13. The bride speaks to the women around her, to those who represent the source of the sufferings that come because of her

fervent desire for greater union with the groom. She compares her beloved to an apple tree among the other trees of the orchard. The key in this comparison, when applied to Christ, is surely that Christ is the image of the tree of life in the Garden of Eden. Through his death on the tree, he has brought forth the abundant fruit of life everlasting to all who wish to eat, not the forbidden fruit of the tree of knowledge, but the fruit of the tree of life.

The bride is seated in the groom's longed-for shade. Christ's Spirit hovers over the bride as love poured out, as the cloud that protects her from the heat of the destructive rays of passions and worldliness. She finds his fruit sweet to her taste. Christ through his sacrifice on the cross has become fruitful in his very death. It is in the Eucharist that his fruit, his very own being, is given to us in the most intimate union possible:

> How good Yahweh is—only taste and see!
> Happy the man who takes shelter in him (Ps 34:8).

To hunger for the fruit from Christ, the tree of life, is to hunger passionately for him, for he is not only the tree but also the fruit. He gives us many graces, but he ardently wishes to give us the greatest gift, himself, as our beloved spouse. We are invited to come and eat of him and have eternal life in him. What greater call to nuptial union than the call to eat of the fruit of this divine tree of life!

14. The groom takes the bride to his banquet hall. In Old Testament understanding, this text refers to the return of the bride of Yahweh, Israel, after the exile to the promised land of Palestine, which is compared to the house of wine (Is 62:8; Jer 31:12). Yahweh's bride will become intoxicated with the wine of divine love.[14] In the new covenant established by the blood of Christ, this sentence has great meaning for the contemplative bride of Christ. After the struggle to overcome sin and other obstacles preventing her from a purer love of Christ, she is led by Christ into the wine cellar, a symbol of intoxication, joy and pleasures, but also of deeper intimacy. The wine with its power to intoxicate symbolizes the Holy Spirit who is given by Christ to his bride after his suffering, death and glorious resurrection.

In the love of Christ that the Spirit pours into the heart of the Christian bride, she experiences a new level of loving union with Christ. He covers her with his banner of love as a conquering general plants his flag and thus claims the territory for his fatherland. In this new and intoxicating experience of love for Christ, the Christian contemplative is almost beside herself with delight bordering on the ecstatic. She is weakened in her own power to control her life, except for the surrendering love she now has for Christ. She is no longer centered on herself. She is sick with love. She can love nothing or no one, but only in and for her groom, Christ.

St. John of the Cross comments on the verse:

> It should be known that many people reach and enter the first wine cellars, each according to the perfection of his love, but few in this life reach this last and most interior, for in it is wrought the perfect union with God, called spiritual marriage, of which the soul is now speaking. What God communicates to the soul in this intimate union is totally beyond words. One can say nothing about it just as one can say nothing about God Himself that resembles Him. For in the transformation of the soul in God, it is God who communicates Himself with admirable glory. In this transformation the two become one, as we would say of the window united with the ray of sunlight, or of the coal with the fire, or of the starlight with the light of the sun. But this union is not as essential and perfect as in the next life.[15]

15. The bride begs to be fed with raisin cakes, to be restored with apples. Both images contain not only a desire to be strengthened in this lovesickness, but they also imply food that would be, according to popular belief of the time, a cure against impotence. The bride is asking for even more love, more fertility coming out of such love. It is a call on her part for greater oneness with Christ, but also that she might forget herself, her smitten condition, and become strengthened to bear fruit. Jesus said to his disciples:

"Whoever remains in me, with me in him,
bears fruit in plenty;
...and I commissioned you
to go out and to bear fruit,
fruit that will last" (Jn 15:5,16).

The Embrace

16. "His left arm is under my head, his right embraces me." The
bride had cried out in her ecstatic joy that the intoxication of her
senses be removed through strengthening "raisin cakes and apples." But the beloved himself comes and embraces her. He places
his left arm under her head and with his right he embraces her.
Christ takes the contemplative, who has entered into swoons of
love that take her out of herself, and supports her in all the trials
and struggles that now confront her.

The embrace with the right arm of Christ can be considered
the spiritual espousal of the bride to Christ, following upon the
trials that he imposes upon her to prepare her for this grace. It
is not the ultimate in transforming union with the groom. It is
the embrace of promise of what is yet to come.

St. Ambrose describes this embrace:

> Happy is the soul who has the good fortune to be so
> embraced by Divine Wisdom! And what great hands
> these are that thus caress and cherish her! They are,
> indeed, hands that embrace the whole soul and that
> encompass and fortify her on every side when she has
> reached the spiritual marriage with the Word of God.
> This is certainly the soul under whose head the Eter-
> nal Wisdom places His left hand, stretching forth His
> right hand so as to embrace her and support her in
> her entire body of works and acts of virtue.[16]

17. The groom orders the daughters of Jerusalem again not to
stir his beloved who has entered into a sleep. She is allowed to
rest until she freely awakes. This statement is found repeated often
and can indicate to us in a mystical interpretation that Christ has
led the bride to a new level of union and she is now resting in
that new awareness as in a healing sleep. How good is Christ,

our spouse, to cover us with such powerful and intoxicating love, to espouse us to him and then allow us in his Spirit to savor the significance of this deeper love until we are ready to undergo the next stages of purification!

Second Poem

(2:8-3:5)

The Bride Speaks

I hear my Beloved.
See how he comes
leaping on the mountains,
bounding over the hills.
My Beloved is like a gazelle,
like a young stag.

See where he stands
behind our wall.
He looks in at the window,
he peers through the lattice.

My Beloved lifts up his voice,
he says to me,
"Come then, my love,
my lovely one, come.
For see, winter is past,
the rains are over and gone.
The flowers appear on the earth.
The season of glad songs has come,
the cooing of the turtledove is heard
in our land.
The fig tree is forming its first figs
and the blossoming vines give out their fragrance.

Come then, my love,
my lovely one, come.
My dove, hiding in the clefts of the rock,
in the coverts of the cliff,
show me your face,
let me hear your voice;
for your voice is sweet

and your face is beautiful."

Catch the foxes for us,
the little foxes
that make havoc of the vineyards,
for our vineyards are in flower.

My Beloved is mine and I am his.
He pastures his flock among the lilies.

Before the dawn-wind rises,
before the shadows flee,
return! Be, my Beloved,
like a gazelle,
a young stag,
on the mountains of the covenant (2:8-17).

1.   The bride is asleep, resting in the love of her spouse. She is asleep to all but her beloved. She is always inwardly attentive to his voice whenever he speaks at night or daytime, in dreams or fully awake, for she knows his voice and wishes to obey his word: "The sheep hear his voice, one by one he calls his own sheep and leads them out...and the sheep follow because they know his voice" (Jn 10:3-4).

2.   She sees him, Christ her beloved, "leaping on the mountains and bounding over the hills." She has experienced God's Word, bounding forth out of the mind of the heavenly Father like a warrior, to enter into a world of darkness, both within her heart and in the heart of the world, and there to conquer the forces of darkness and evil. Her beloved, now in his resurrectional presence, comes leaping over all heights, from the mountains to the hills, even to the valleys of her own inner poverty and brokenness, to bring his healing love. His resurrectional presence brings to the Christian a transcendence that cannot be limited to any space or time. Truly, Christ lifts up his bride and shares with her his ability to transcend all physical limitations and to live even now in eternal life.

3.   Christ, the beloved, is compared to a gazelle and a young stag. In his resurrection he is given a newness of life, of power, of swiftness to be wherever the bride calls out to him. He has con-

quered the powers of death (Rv 1:18) and holds the keys of death and of the underworld. With the swiftness of a gazelle and the endurance of a young stag, the risen Lord comes bounding into the life of the one who calls on his name.

4. The bride sees him standing behind "our" wall, meaning that he wishes to share himself most intimately with his bride, but at this stage of union he appears outside of her humanity. The mystical marriage is yet to come, a union which will no longer keep him on the "outside." Jesus is always present outside and within us, yet we fail to see him as present and loving us with perfect, passionate love unto death. Origen compares the window to the physical senses of the contemplative who attains to her spouse through sense knowledge. The beloved "peers through the lattice," for he wishes to give himself to his beloved in a way she can receive his loving presence. Thus Origen explains this passage:

> But that He is said to "look through the nets" of the windows doubtless points to the fact that so long as the soul is in the house of this body, she cannot receive the naked and plain wisdom of God, but beholds the invisible and the incorporeal by means of certain analogies and token and images of visible things. And this is what is meant by the Bridegroom looking at her through the nets of the window.[17]

Christ stands on that level where the bride is and looks in to beckon her to break out of her "enclosure" of security in her relationship with him and to follow him in greater freedom and more intimate union.

Come, My Love

1. Now Christ, the beloved, speaks to his beloved and summons her to come and follow him. He calls her, "my love, my lovely one," for she is already pleasing to him. But it is a call to come out of herself. Earlier the groom bade her to forget herself insofar as she yearned inordinately for the delights he brought her. Now she has obeyed him in undergoing trials and sufferings in the purification of the senses. He calls her to come forth to labor even

51

more diligently to bring forth fruit of the new life that he has espoused himself to give her through his resurrectional presence.

St. Augustine writes beautifully of the ways in which Christ calls us individually according to our development and disposition:

> O God, the strength of my salvation! I go astray and You call to me over and over again; I resist You and You invite me; I am idle and You rouse me; I am converted and You embrace me; I am ignorant and You instruct me; I am sad and You cheer me; I fall and You lift me up; You restore me after the fall; You give me all I ask You for; You let me find You when I look for You and You open the door when I call. So that, Lord God of my life, I do not know what excuse I could have. Now, Father of mercies and God of all consolation,...grant me the joy of Your countenance that by loving You I might receive all that You promised me...inspire me as to what I must think of You, teach me what words I must use to invoke You and give me works with which to please You.[18]

2. "For see, winter is past, the rains are over and gone." Winter is a sign here of the many trials of coldness, darkness and a sense of being close to death. There have been the spiritual rains, coldness and snow abounding in the bride's experiences of her beloved. There have been the lifelessness of winter sins that have gripped her and throttled to death that loving presence of Christ to her. Now Christ calls to her that all such "passive diminishments" on the spiritual level are gone. Through his new life in the resurrection he puts an end to fears. "Fear not; it is I!" Nothing outside is life-giving, the bride is beginning to realize, except the love of Christ. Nothing outside can bring worry, fear or anxiety to her, for he is now with her in a new and more permanent way.

3. "The flowers appear on the earth. The season of glad songs has come, the cooing of the turtledove is heard in our land." He calls this "our" land to which he wants to bring her, the bride, and there to enjoy a deeper share in the life he has won for her through his death and resurrection. Flowers are found everywhere,

not like the lilies of the field that fade away and lose their short-lived beauty, but these flowers will last forever. She need fear no longer the coming of winter and death. This is the new spring. It is time for celebration and joyous songs such as are sung at weddings, because he is calling her to enter into such new life by a nuptial union. The cooing of the turtledove is heard, a sign of lovemaking. The dove symbolizes the groom's simplicity and purity, which only exists to enable him to give himself in self-sacrificing love.

4. The symbols of figs and vines further the theme of spring and the bursting forth of new life, with fruit produced out of suffering. The fig was often used by Jewish commentators to indicate the fruitful development of a woman, and thus they applied this symbol to Israel. A girl is like an unripe fig that is still green; a maiden is in the early stages of ripening, whereas the mother is fully ripened. Figs begin to develop as fruit, the first signs after winter. Vines blossom before they bring forth their grapes. They must be pruned to bring forth abundant fruit (Jn 15:1). The contemplative possesses the fullness of fruit in the early stages of the spiritual life. But the fruit needs development under the guiding hand of the fruit grower.

Come Then, My Love

1. Again the spouse repeats his earlier phrase: "Come then, my love, my lovely one, come." He is calling his beloved to come forth out of her hiding in the clefts of the rock, in the coverts of the cliff. He wishes her to come to him in a new, surrendering way. How can he call her to come since he has never left her, except to call her out of her focus on self? He wishes her to leave the contentment she finds in being recollected within herself in order to find her complete happiness in him. Leaving herself is like the death of winter. Coming to her beloved and surrendering more totally to his loving union is to bring spring into summer and full harvest.

2. The groom wishes the bride to show him her face. He desires to hear her voice, for "your voice is sweet and your face is beautiful." Christ sees us as most beautiful, regardless of whether we are in the winter, spring, summer or harvest of the spiritual

life. He wishes to hear our voice praising him and his Father through the fullness of the Holy Spirit, who prays within us when we do not know how to pray as we ought (Rom 8:26). He already sees our radiant faces as they will become if only we surrender and come to him in full union. If you and I knew how beautiful we are already, our true faces turned in loving surrender to Christ, how sweet our voice would always be saying: "Be it done unto me according to thy word." We would never hide in the clefts of the rock of loneliness again, but only in the rock that is Christ. This was the thought of St. Paul when he wrote: "All ate the same spiritual food and all drank the same spiritual drink, since they all drank from the spiritual rock that followed them as they went, and that rock was Christ" (1 Cor 10:3-4).

3.   The Spirit reveals to us, as St. Paul writes, that the Israelites in the desert drank from the spiritual rock which followed them as they went, "and that rock was Christ" (1 Cor 10:3-4). Mystics throughout all of Christianity are led to come out of themselves and enter into the pierced heart of Christ and there to have the exchange of "hearts," where two consciousnesses are made one. Jesus' side was pierced by a soldier's spear and from the heart of Jesus, St. John the beloved disciple notes, there flowed water and blood. This detail reveals not only the *kenotic* (emptying) love of Jesus and his Father for us, bought at a great price; it is also a revelation in symbol that the dying Jesus is now glorified by being empowered by his Father to send us his Holy Spirit. A whole school of exegesis, including such teachers as Ignatius Martyr, Polycarp, Irenaeus, Hippolytus and John Chrysostom, has interpreted this saying of Jesus to indicate that from his breast (or heart) shall flow "fountains of living water."[19]

The Spirit is the living water that in baptism comes to us from the pierced heart of Jesus. Jesus is the Lamb that is slain (Rv 5:12). The Spirit purifies our hearts, the deepest layers of consciousness, by revealing the love of Jesus for us in the symbol of his pierced heart. Contemplating the depths of his love for us, we are cleansed of self-centeredness. We can continuously approach this sacred fountain, the rock that is Jesus Christ, and be washed in the water and blood of Christ.

The Spirit gives us an exchange of hearts as foretold by Ezekiel (Ez 36:26-29). Through the Spirit we can recognize Jesus as the Lamb of God who takes away our sins (Jn 1:29). We proclaim that Jesus is "the Lamb who is at the throne (who) will be their shepherd and will lead them to springs of living water"(Rv 7:17). The river of life, the Spirit, rises from the throne of God and from the Lamb (Rv 22:1).

> The spirit and the Bride say, "Come." Let everyone who listens, answer "Come." Then let all who are thirsty come: all who want it may have the water of life, and have it free (Rv 22:17).

It is certainly the Holy Spirit who has revealed to mystics down through the ages as they contemplated the pierced heart of God on the cross, that from the side of Christ, the New Adam, we, the church, the spouse of Christ, the new Eve, are brought into life.[20]

You and I also can enter into the heart of Christ, our bridegroom, and experience in the cleft of the rock, Christ, how beautiful we have become by his redeeming love. As St. Paul reflects:

> Christ loved the Church and sacrificed himself for her to make her holy. He made her clean by washing her in water with a form of words, so that when he took her to himself she would be glorious, with no speck or wrinkle or anything like that, but holy and faultless (Eph 5:25-27).

We can daily experience in prayer what it means to enter into the "heart" of Jesus Christ, into the depths of his conscious, sacrificing love for each of us, and in that perfect love we can be reborn of his Spirit. St. John Chrysostom beautifully comments on the wounded side of Christ where we can enter as he calls us to come and be made beautiful in his love:

> The lance of the soldier opened the side of Christ, and behold...from his wounded side Christ built the Church, as once the first mother, Eve, was formed

from Adam. Hence Paul says: Of his flesh we are and of his bond. By that he means the wounded side of Jesus. As God took the rib out of Adam's side and from it formed the woman, so Christ gives us water and blood from his wounded side and forms from it the Church...there the slumber of Adam; here the death-sleep of Jesus.[21]

The Little Foxes

1. The groom exhorts his bride that with his help she is to catch the little foxes who are causing havoc to the vineyards, which are already in flower. Who are these little foxes that pose such a threat to the vineyards? Origen in his commentary claimed they were the heretics who attacked the bride-church of Christ. The fox is depicted in most popular fables in world literature as the most clever, elusive and deceitful of animals. Jesus called King Herod a fox because of his deceitfulness (Lk 13:32).

The grown foxes eat the full-grown fruit, but the little foxes nibble at the flowers. There will be no fruit if the flowers and the beginning of fruit on the vines are destroyed by such little foxes. We can see that the groom is calling the bride to her responsibility to guard against any movement of the heart that would allow any destructive force to enter into their love relationship. Jesus had taught how subtle is the heart of human beings: "It is what comes out of a man that makes him unclean. For it is from within, from men's hearts, that evil intentions emerge: fornication, theft, murder, adultery, avarice, malice, deceit, indecency, envy, slander, pride, folly. All these evil things come from within and make a man unclean" (Mk 7:21-23).

There can be no growth in union with Jesus Christ without vigilance in controlling one's thoughts. Jesus calls us to constant vigilance and. inner discipline. St. Paul challenged his early Christian converts to bring into captivity and under obedience to Jesus Christ every thought and every imagination (2 Cor 10:5). Such movements of the heart may seem not very big or important to an outsider. But for one who truly loves Christ every thought will be weighed militantly to see whether or not it brings the beloved closer to Christ.

Yet we know that without Christ we can do nothing (Jn 15:5). He promises to be always with us, to help us to abide in him and thus bear great fruit (Jn 15:5). St. John teaches us that we possess within us one who is more powerful than any enemy outside: "Children, you have already overcome these false prophets, because you are from God and you have in you one who is greater than anyone in this world" (1 Jn 4:4).

My Beloved Is Mine

1.   The groom had called to his bride to enter into a new death-resurrection experience, to leap with him on the mountains after leaving the narrow enclosure of her heart where she had first met her spouse in affective union. The bride seemingly does not answer his call to come and enter into deeper purification because she is inordinately attached to the delights from his loving presence. The focus is on herself as she maintains that her beloved belongs to her and that she is his. She wants more sweetness of oneness with him, but has not heeded his call to move away from her own self-interest in order to live totally for him. Here is a crucial turning point in union with Christ: to be attached to one's own interests, to use Christ for one's own feeling of well-being and not to be inwardly attentive to such "little foxes" or spiritual attachments that destroy any greater intimacy with him.

2.   She sees Christ as pasturing his flock among the lilies. She considers herself as one among the lilies by her purity in wanting to belong totally to him. She sees what he is to her, what he does to her that makes her special above others. Yet she is still focused upon herself and not upon Christ. She has ignored his call to leave herself and enter into a freedom through putting to death every subtle feeling of attachment to Christ for what he can do for her. She continues to dwell on his sweetness.

3.   She is on her bed in the night, crying out to him to come back. She wants him in the absence she feels during the night, during the purifications that have come upon her, "before the dawn-wind rises, before the shadows flee," before a new day of oneness dawns: She wants him now. She wants her beloved to be like a gazelle, a young stag, to return in great haste so she does not have

to suffer through this dark night of his absence. Yet the wise and good shepherd knows what is good for his sheep. He seemingly leaves her in order that she may rise up from her self-centeredness and set off to find him outside her own self-seeking.

Chapter Three

The Bride:

On my bed, at night, I sought him
whom my heart loves.
I sought but did not find him.
So I will rise and go through the City;
in the streets and the squares
I will seek him whom my heart loves.
...I sought but did not find him.

The watchmen came upon me
on their rounds in the City:
"Have you seen him whom my heart loves?"

Scarcely had I passed them
than I found him whom my heart loves.
I held him fast, nor would I let him go
till I had brought him
into my mother's house,
into the room of her who conceived me.

The Bridegroom:

I charge you,
daughters of Jerusalem,
by the gazelles, by the hinds of the field,
not to stir my love, nor rouse it,
until it please to awake (3:1-5).

I Shall Arise and Seek Him

1.   The bride complains that she has sought her beloved on her bed at night, through many nights, but she did not find him. He no longer appears to her in ecstatic sentiments. She seeks him inordinately as she sought him before in feelings and consolations

that gave her certitude of his love for her. Now, in nights of his absence, she is tortured in agony. She is being called into a deeper transformation in loving union with Christ, her spouse, but first she must pass through the necessary purification of her heart of all self-centeredness.

If you have begun to make progress in the spiritual life, you will come to realize what this series of "nights" mean. Such purification is a call to go deeper into your "heart," the scriptural symbol of deepest consciousness, in self-surrendering love to Christ as your supreme lover. Beyond all preconditionings of your false self, your past training, thought patterns, even sins, you are called by Christ to enter deeper and deeper into your consciousness and to claim new areas of conquest in the dark recesses of your unconscious. You push in prayerful encounter with Christ through the various strata of emotions and affections, beyond the confinement of fixity arranged comfortably into a *status quo* of heredity, social relationships, and former prayer experiences.

With God's grace and indwelling presence you are in search of your true self in loving union with Christ as you elect to participate in God's shared nature (2 Pt 1:4). There is so much more of you to come into being, if you have the courage to enter into the interior battle. God is calling you constantly into a process of letting go of the controlled activity you have been exercising in your prayer life. You stand on the fringe of the barren desert. Now Christ is calling you to let go of your controlled thinking, fantasizing about him and yourself in mental dialogue, and to surrender in deeper faith, hope and love to his indwelling presence, beyond any feeling you may have. Your spouse, Christ, is calling you into deeper darkness, the darkening of your own rational knowledge, to enter into a new way of receiving the communication of himself in the "luminous darkness" of faith. It is to say goodbye to the protection of self-made props that may have served you well on a lower level of beginning prayer.

St. Bernard explains this search for the hidden spouse and God's strategy in bringing the contemplative into the purification of the night of his absence:

> The Spouse did not return at the Bride's cries un-
> doubtedly so as to quicken her desires, to try her af-

fection and to enkindle her more and more in divine love. These trials are more the product of pretense than indignation. They are stratagems to make the soul continue seeking Him, for although He was called He did not come. Perhaps if He is sought after He will allow Himself to be found as it is promised in the Gospel (Mt 7:8): Search and you will find....Enkindled in greater desires to find her Beloved, the loving Bride goes out in search of Him with all the ardor of her soul. She searches for Him first of all in the bed and in no way can find Him....And it should be noted that she has not gone out vainly searching for Him on just one occasion, on just one night; for she tells us that many were the sleepless nights she spent looking for him.[22]

I Sought But Did Not Find Him

1. The searching for Christ can be done only by the individual, for intimacy is between two persons. On the negative side, such searching, such ascetical vigilance to uproot any inordinate, passionate desire to find Christ as we would wish him to come to us "on our bed" of pleasure and delight, brings with it the necessity of ridding ourselves of any compulsive behavior, of any "thoughtless" self-indulgence in thought, word or deed. Such preconditioning actions or thoughts bind us in a slavery to senses or internal faculties of emotions, imagination, memory, intellect or will that take us away from our being centered in loving obedience upon Christ. To become Christ-conscious more and more of one's complete life must be under God's will.

Fragmentation toward every desire that impedes inner attention and oneness with Christ must be corrected by inner vigilance. This is the work of what St. John of the Cross describes as the night of the senses. It is the withdrawal of deliberate desire from the objects of inordinate sense satisfaction by creating a greater desire for Christ and for union with him. Such going against our human nature, conditioned to act without reference to God's holy will in every thought, word and deed, will always bring about a certain suffering. But Christian hope lies in the necessary therapy of such suffering leading to a greater sharing in Christ's resurrected life.

2. Yet Christ, your beloved spouse, actively enters into the purification of your attachments to sense delights in your love for him. It is your degree of free and joyful surrendering to Christ's purifying hand that will determine whether or not you will make any progress in contemplative prayer. Christ calls you to "leap on the mountains, bounding over the hills" with him by the relinquishing of your control over him in prayerful union. He cannot break through with a more immediate and direct manner of communicating himself to you through deepening faith, hope and love as long as you are in control of the prayerful dialogue between yourself and him.

Spiritual delights may have been yours in earlier stages of prayer. You may so easily seek Christ on your bed, in your ease and comfort, and become confused in desiring the gifts of God more than God himself. Christ withdraws himself from appearing to you in such sweetness so that you may not become attached to feeling in prayer and think it the same as true love. Christ's purifying you begins by his throwing you into utter aridity, into night after night of searching for his presence. No longer are you flooded with sensible feelings of his presence and his love for you.

The first sign of such purification through aridity, as St. John of the Cross teaches,[23] is that you do not receive satisfaction or consolation from the things of God, or from any other creatures either. Another sign of this purification brought to you through the workings of Christ is that you sense with keener awareness your own powerlessness to find God in prayer of any kind. There is only night!

So I Will Rise

1. How beautiful is the power that God places within your will to choose to direct your life to higher levels of self-forgetfulness and to greater love of God! The Prodigal Son (Lk 15:17-20) said the right words as he rose from the husks of swine to return to his father. The bride becomes aware that she has been selfishly seeking her beloved in a rest that was self-seeking. It was on "her" bed that she sought him. Earlier the groom had said that "our bed is green" (1:16-17). Now the bride in sorrow rises from her bed and goes out into the city, into the streets and the squares to seek her beloved.

The city stands for Jerusalem, the image of the heavenly city where the Lamb of God will reign supreme over all creation. The bride seeks within the context of the church and its means of mediating Christ and his grace to the faithful. She had earlier sought him through the teachings of church leaders, through the sacraments, and in the fellowship of a worshipping community and had found him. Now she returns to such fellowship but even there she does not discover him, not even as she did before.

2.   She turns to the watchmen on their rounds in the city and she asks: "Have you seen him whom my heart loves?" These are the true teachers in the church who earlier had helped her to find him. She does not have to mention his name, for these teachers live for exalting Christ. But they no longer are able to help her find him "whom her heart loves."

I Found Him Whom My Heart Loves

1.   The bride had seen that the watchmen could not help her. No sooner did she pass by them in her haste to find her beloved than she says: "I found him whom my heart loves. I held him fast, nor would I let him go till I had brought him into my mother's house, into the room of her who conceived me." How true it is that if we sincerely seek to find the Lord, he will come to us. He reads our hearts and sees whether we are honest and pure in heart. The bride underwent the many nights of purification that led her away from her own self-seeking to reach a point where she was ready to let go and surrender on a new level of commitment to her beloved.

At this point Christ appears to you, bringing you the promise of a greater union following your self-emptying. He will take you into a betrothal unto his own. It does not mean the end of purification. It means that he allows you to rest in this newly found oneness with him.

2.   We read those beautiful words: "I held him fast, nor would I let him go..., " knowing that now Christ's bride is holding on to Christ with even greater tenacity, but also greater detachment

from her own self-holding. Like Jacob, she has wrestled with God in darkness: "I will not let you go unless you bless me" (Gn 32:28). She has been purified of her own self-seeking and now can say with the psalmist:

> I look to no one else in heaven,
> I delight in nothing else on earth.
> My flesh and my heart are pining with love,
> my heart's Rock, my own, God for ever! (Ps 73:25-26).

3.   Through deeper and purer faith she clings now to her beloved. She will not let him go until she leads him into her mother's house into the room of her mother who conceived her. Here is the image of the contemplative returning with the groom into her mother's house, the church, which by Christ's power and grace has conceived the bride into God's very own life. She returns to the beginning and, in the words of T.S. Eliot: "And the end of all our exploring will be to arrive where we started. And know the place for the first time."[24]
    Part of her purification is to realize how important is Mother Church and all her teachings, inspired by the Holy Spirit, Christ's gift to his body. When the bride is no longer the criterion of her attachment to Christ, the norms put down by the church in keeping with God's Word become all important. She turns to the church and recognizes that it is there she will be able to enter into ever greater union with Christ and no longer to fear herself as the source of illusion.

The Bridegroom Speaks (3:5)

    The bridegroom ends this section with the similar injunction he gave to the daughters of Jerusalem, to allow his beloved not to be roused or disturbed in her new oneness with him until she awakes herself. Christ allows us to come out of night and purification into a new union with him and there to remain in peace and divine resting without any disturbance from those who are found in a lower union with him.

Third Poem

What is this coming up from the desert
like a column of smoke,
breathing of myrrh and frankincense
and every perfume the merchant knows?

See, it is the litter of Solomon.
Around it are sixty champions,
the flower of the warriors of Israel;
all of them skilled swordsmen,
veterans of battle.
Each man has his sword at his side,
against alarms by night.

King Solomon
has made himself a throne
of wood from Lebanon.
The posts he has made of silver,
the canopy of gold,
the seat of purple,
the back is inlaid with ebony.

Daughters of Zion,
come and see
King Solomon,
wearing the diadem with which his mother crowned
    him
on his wedding day,
on the day of his heart's joy

1. This love poem begins with those standing by, probably the
daughters of Jerusalem, who are not as advanced as the bride in

her purified love and oneness with her beloved, amazed at the sight of her coming out of the desert. Through the desert of faith she comes like a column of smoke. God first led his chosen people over the Red Sea and into the purifications of the desert under the column of fire, a sign of the guidance of the Holy Spirit (Ex 13:22). In the second exile Yahweh leads his people, his bride Israel, back to Jerusalem, as Isaiah writes:

> Yahweh will come and rest
> on the whole stretch of Mount Zion
> and on those who are gathered there,
> a cloud by day, and smoke,
> and by night the brightness of a flaring fire (Is 4:5).

The bride is seen by the daughters as covered by God's Holy Spirit, filled with the fire of divine love. She breathes myrrh and frankincense, which refer to Christ, both in his passion, sufferings and death, but also in his new life that gives off a fragrance such as myrrh and frankincense do and "every perfume" known to merchants. The bride has not only learned the lesson, but the sufferings she has undergone have given her a share in the new life with the risen Lord. She has experienced the fulfillment of St. Paul's prayer: "All I want is to know Christ and the power of his resurrection and to share his sufferings by reproducing the pattern of his death. That is the way I can hope to take my place in the resurrection of the dead" (Phil 3:10-11).

King Solomon

1.   In answer to their own question, the daughters of Jerusalem see the litter of Solomon approaching from the desert. It is surrounded by 60 outstanding warriors of Israel, skilled swordsmen, veterans of battle. Each is armed with a sword at his side to protect the king and his bride from the "alarms" of the night. Commentators have brought no end of interpretations to this text.

Solomon has given his palanquin or Oriental-covered conveyance to carry his bride. All the images signify a groom taking his bride to himself in solemn procession after the wedding. Simple Oriental peoples feared evil demons on the night of the wedding at the time of consumating a marriage in sexual union.

Hence guards against the alarms by night were posted to prevent such evil spirits from inflicting harm upon the newly-weds.[25]

In a mystical, Christian interpretation we see Solomon as Christ, Wisdom incarnate of the Father, who has won his bride by dying for her. He is the Messiah who has risen from the dead. He wishes to give himself completely to his bride in mystical marriage. He surrounds his nuptial bed with 60 warriors who stand for those giants of the faith in the Old and New Testaments who through the scriptures protect the bride against any disruptive enemies.

2.   The daughters describe Solomon's throne: made of wood from Lebanon; posts made of silver with a canopy of gold, and a seat of purple with the back inlaid with ebony. This throne is Christ himself in his risen glory, which becomes the nuptial seat for the bride and himself now one in transforming union. The throne is made out of wood from Lebanon, which was considered to be incorruptible. Christ's risen body is now incorruptible, and we Christians are called to share in his incorruptible body. He calls us into the most intimate union with him to share in eternal life. We are his body. St. Paul captures this reality when he writes:

> A man never hates his own body, but he feeds it and looks after it; and that is the way Christ treats the Church, because it is his body—and we are its living parts.... This mystery has many implications; but I am saying it applies to Christ and the Church (Eph 5:29-32).

The pillars of this throne are made of silver, which depicts the humanity through which he redeemed us. Thus the strength of these pillars consists in not only Christ's humanity, but that humanity exalted in glory and made one with his divinity so that we who are totally human can be given a share in his divinity through his redemption. Against such pillars of strength no power, not even hell, can prevail. No one can touch you, no force outside can ever take you from the love of Christ (Rom 8:39).

Overhead is a canopy of gold which symbolizes that he, Christ, is divine, of the same substance with the Father. Our redemption stands on the fundamental reality that God in the humanity of Christ suffered and died: We are saved by God's infinite love poured out on the cross, God truly dying for us.

His seat is of purple signifying royalty. Christ through his resurrection has been raised up by the Father in glory and has been given the name of *Kyrios*, Lord of the universe. He rules over all. He is the *Pantocrator*, the one who is almighty over every kingdom, including the kingdom of sin and death. We should have to fear no one, knowing that this king is our spouse who lives within us (1 Jn 4:4).

The back of the throne is covered with ebony. In Hebrew the correct word should be "love." This love goes out for the daughters of Jerusalem, for Christ's bride, his church, for the individual Christian to whom he wishes to wed himself.

3. If this throne is a picture of Jesus Christ, it is also a picture of what he does to his bride. He gives himself to her. She sits on the throne, for by his healing love she has become what he is. She is made incorruptible, like wood from Lebanon. Her supports are made of silver through the redeeming humanity of her groom. His gold and purple, his divinity and kingship, are shared with her. The covering of the back of the throne is of love for his loved one.

The Approaching Wedding Day

1. The bride, overwhelmed by the riches given to her through her king-spouse, invites the daughters of Zion, those less advanced than she, to come and see her beloved, the king of wisdom and of peace. She points him out to them, he wearing the crown his mother crowned him with on his wedding day. We can easily see the symbol in the Old Testament understanding of this passage: Yahweh taking his people to himself in a mystical marriage as his long-awaited bride.

But in our Christian interpretation, the bride encourages other Christians to come and see the king who is her beloved.

> Turn to me and be saved,
> all the ends of the earth,
> for I am God unrivalled (Is 45:22).

Jesus had asked others to look up at him hanging on the cross, crowned not with a regal diadem made out of gems and precious gold, but with a crown of thorns, and to accept him as their king-spouse.

> "...and the Son of Man must be lifted up
> as Moses lifted up the serpent in the desert,
> so that everyone who believes may have eternal life
> in him" (Jn 3:13-14).

Christ's day of espousal was his death on the cross of Calvary. Out of his side came forth his bride, the church. You and I have been born out of his pierced side through the outpouring of the Holy Spirit in water and blood, through the regenerating sacraments of baptism and Eucharist. You became the bride of Christ on Calvary through the Holy Spirit. St. Paul understood how all of us through baptism and Eucharist are called to be the bride of Christ: "I arranged for you to marry Christ so that I might give you away as as chaste virgin to this one husband" (2 Cor 11:2).

Christ's wedding day, when his mother Mary crowned him with the humanity that reached its fullness on Calvary, is the day of his "heart's joy" (3:11). We tend to ponder the sufferings of Christ on the cross, but we do not always understand that this was his hour, the joyful sacrifice waited for all his earthly existence. It was for this that he became man and dwelt among us, in order that he might be crowned king of the world as your individual bridegroom.

Chapter Four

The Bridegroom

> How beautiful you are, my love,
> how beautiful you are!
> Your eyes, behind your veil,
> are doves;
> your hair is like a flock of goats
> frisking down the slopes of Gilead.

Your teeth are like a flock of shorn ewes
as they come up from the washing.
Each one has its twin,
not one unpaired with another.
Your lips are a scarlet thread
and your words enchanting.
Your cheeks, behind your veil,
are halves of pomegranate.
Your neck is the tower of David
built as a fortress,
hung round with a thousand bucklers,
and each the shield of a hero.
Your two breasts are two fawns,
twins of a gazelle,
that feed among the lilies.

Before the dawn-wind rises,
before the shadows flee,
I will go to the mountain of myrrh,
to the hill of frankincense.

You are wholly beautiful, my love.
and without a blemish.

Come from Lebanon, my promised bride,
come from Lebanon, come on your way.
Lower your gaze, from the heights of Amana,
from the crests of Senir and Hermon,
the haunt of lions,
the mountains of leopards (4:1-8).

1. The bridegroom has espoused himself to his bride after her purifications and he begins to praise her for her beauty. He repeats what he said about her in 1:15, but most of this chapter consists of images upon images to describe the new life and beauty that shine forth from the bride, who now is living in a new oneness with her beloved.

Her eyes are compared to those of doves as they hide behind her veil. The dove in Christian thought is an image of the Holy Spirit. The bride has progressed through sufferings and a process of confronting her own self-centeredness to a purer love of her spouse. The Holy Spirit brings her an increase of his fruit: "love, joy, peace, patience, kindness, goodness, trustfulness, gentleness and self-control" (Gal 5:22). In one word, the dove speaks of the new simplification of the bride's life around her beloved. She lives no longer for herself, but it is Christ who is the center of the contemplative's life (Gal 2:20). She acts with no deviousness, but only with a single eye to give pleasure to her beloved. There is only sincerity in her dealings with Christ and her neighbors. She is spontaneous and free to live solely out of love, cost what that may in terms of self-sacrifice, for simplicity has come to her through the "pass-over" experience of death to her own self to live only for the loved one.

2.   Her hair is like a flock of goats frisking down the slopes of Gilead. This refers to the Syrian goat with its long, silky, black hair. Here it is a whole flock together to which the bride is compared in the beauty of her hair. St. Paul speaks of a woman's hair: "...woman, who was given her hair as a covering, thinks long hair her glory" (1 Cor 11:15). The bride's long, freely flowing hair represents her freed spirit under the love of her groom in obedience and submission to him. This is her glory now, to obey her beloved in every detail of her life, in her thoughts, imaginations, words and deeds. When Samson had his hair cut by Delilah through his carnal attachment to her and in violation of God's law, he lost God's favor. All his inner and external strengths were also lost. He went out into darkness, for his eyes had been put out (Jg 16:16-22). The bride is complimented by Christ for her complete submission to him in keeping all his commandments (Jn 14:23). To obey Christ is truly to reign with him.

How Beautiful You Are, My Love

3.   Now the groom describes the bride's beauty by a series of comparisons of her teeth, lips, cheeks, neck and breasts. We should keep in mind that in Semitic thought, external beauty was considered a reflection of some internal attribute that could not be seen or manifested except in comparison to what externally seemed to be harmonious and beautiful to the physical eyes of the beholder. Her teeth, become strong and straight and white by masticating the spiritual food provided her by Christ, are lik-

ened to a flock of shorn ewes as they come up from washing. Before the wool was cut from the sheep, the sheep were waded through water to clean the wool. The bride has been cleansed by the water through the word of God (Eph 5:26). And, though her sins may have been red as crimson, she has now become white as wool. Each sheep has its twin, implying the fertility that has come to the bride by her chewing spiritual food and being careful of what she eats: "Do not let yourselves be led astray by all sorts of strange doctrines: it is better to rely on grace for inner strength than on dietary laws which have done no good to those who kept them" (Heb 13:9).

4.   Her lips are a scarlet thread and her words enchanting. Such lips are a sign of health: a beautiful line of scarlet, lips that are full of life and health. The prophet Isaiah saw himself as one with unclean lips: "I am lost, for I am a man of unclean lips and I live among a people of unclean lips" (Is 6:5). But Yahweh cleansed his lips and his iniquity was taken away and his sin purged (Is 6:7). The bride enjoys spiritual health, for the blood of her beloved has cleansed her of any sinfulness and now has given her beauty of soul and body. Through such lips her words become enchanting to the groom and to others who hear her speak. The psalmist echoes this comparison:

> Of all men you are the most handsome,
> your lips are moist with grace,
> for God has blessed you for ever (Ps 45:2).

Now that she is espoused to her beloved, her lips and her speech are even more attractive and enticing, for she wishes to use them only to exalt Christ.

5.   Her cheeks behind her veil are halves of pomegranate. The pomegranate when cut reveals white seeds covered with a crimson fluid. She is pure and spotless in her commitment to her groom, yet the sign of his death, his blood, covers her and makes her even more beautiful, for she lives to share in his sufferings as to share also in his glory (Rom 8:17).

6.   The neck of the bride is compared to the strong tower of David, built like a fortress, which is ringed with a thousand

bucklers, each a shield of a hero. Her straight neck is beautiful in being connected to the head, Christ. She is not a stiff-necked person, stubborn to follow her own will, but is supple and directly under obedience to the head. She has been set free by Christ and now is a woman, selected by God, as David was (Acts 13:22), to be after his own heart.

The Shield of Faith

The bride is engaged in a spiritual war, but Christ has made her into a tower of strength, like the impregnable citadel of King David. She has a thousand bucklers hanging on her tower. St. Paul exhorts the Christian to always carry "the shield of faith so that you can use it to put out the burning arrows of the evil one. And then you must accept salvation from God to be your helmet and receive the word of God from the Spirit to use as a sword" (Eph 6:16-17). The bride's faith has been tested in the purification of her senses and for this her beloved praises her deeper faith, ready to follow him in sickness and in health, in humiliations and in joy, in life or death.

She is surrounded in her faith by the faith of a thousand warriors, "mighty men" of faith, who have helped her build her faith upon their heroic exploits in following God in complete abandonment. These were people Abel (Heb 11:4), Enoch, Noah, Abraham, Isaac, Jacob, Moses, Rahab the prostitute, Gideon, Barak, Samson, David, Samuel and the prophets. "These were men, who through faith conquered kingdoms, did what is right and earned the promises" (Heb 11:33). And she in her interior battle against her false self proved herself no less heroic as she used the shield of faith to ward off any enemies that attacked the life of God within her.

7.   Her breasts are like young twin roes or fawns who feed among the lilies. Symbolically, breasts are the scriptural *heart*, the seat of all affections, especially of love. Her breasts of faith and love are evenly balanced. In exercising faith and love, the two commandments are evenly balanced also: to love God with all her heart and to love her neighbor as she loves herself. The lilies show her purity of conscience as she returns Christ's love to him without any guilt or guile.

Prayer and Sacrifice

8. The groom breaks off his description of the bride's enchanting beauty. Before the daylight of consolations or greater union takes place, he will go off to the mountain of myrrh and to the hill of frankincense. Myrrh is the symbol of suffering, of mortifications that lead to a dying of self. Frankincense is what the Magi offered to the Christ-child at Bethlehem as a sign of his divinity. It is a sign of prayerful lifting of oneself to God in adoration:

> My prayers rise like incense,
> My hands like the evening offering (Ps 141:2).

The mountain and hill recall Jerusalem and the Temple on Mt. Moriah, where God is adored in prayer and sacrifice by his chosen people.

The groom is saying that, although the bride is so ravishing in inner and exterior beauty, there is more to come. If she wishes to have a part with him and to enter into greater beauty and oneness with him, she needs to ascend with him the mountain of self-sacrifice and the hill of worshipful prayer.

Without Blemish

1. The groom seems unable to contain himself in praise of his beautiful bride as he repeats what he had said earlier: "You are wholly beautiful, my love," but now adds: "...and without a blemish." After each purification and new level of oneness with him, the bride becomes more beautiful. How humbled the bride must be to hear these words addressed to her by her beloved!

She had cooperated through long "nights" of purification. She has shown courage and constancy in her fidelity to follow her groom in obedience. The life of the Holy Spirit has taken root in her and has blossomed forth in a beautiful array of virtues. She humbly knows that it is all God's work of grace, which he has freely bestowed upon her. She magnifies the Lord for all he has done in her life. She sees clearly that this is due to the love of her beloved, drawing her through tribulations and trials to experience his great love for her.

Yet, even though Christ sees no blemish in her, she is humbled by human defects that show she is not completely as she ought to be. How God gently keeps us from imputing evil to such human imperfections by not even regarding them as obstacles to union with him! She is still in need of purification, but now, through the deep, positive love she has received in her betrothal to her beloved, she knows such defects and failures are not deliberate and sinful but are helpful means to attain even greater union and beauty before Christ.

Come, My Bride

1.   Here for the first time the bridegroom calls his beloved his "bride." He has espoused her as his own. Yet the bride still needs to come down to him, away from the mountains of Lebanon and the heights of Amaña, Senir and Hermon, all territories foreign to the groom's land. This is a call to the bride to receive his offer to become mystically united in transforming union. How the soul must thrill at what she so eagerly wants! Yet how realistically is Christ, our spouse, who calls us to greater union by summoning us away from the mountains that not only separate us from him but possess inimical forces that could destroy us.

The bride needs to take only the final step to receive what her heart so ardently desires—complete consummation in nuptial union with her beloved. Yet Christ warns her, not teasingly but realistically, that she must flee from such distant heights, filled with lions and leopards that could so easily destroy her. Although the groom is with her, yet in spirit she is still far away, inhabiting a foreign land filled with forces that threaten her very existence.

She herself does not suspect the many obstacles that lie within herself, within the layers of her consciousness and above all her unconscious. She truly wants to belong completely to Christ. She believes in what St. Paul called putting on the "new self" in Christ: "Your mind must be renewed by a spiritual revolution so that you can put on the new self that has been created in God's way, in the goodness and holiness of the truth" (Eph 4:23-24).

Jesus was driven into the desert by the Holy Spirit (Mk 1:12). This has been for Christians throughout all ages the model for "returning to one's true self," the way to reach transforming union with Christ by entering into one's heart and there doing battle against crippling, demonic forces, the "lions" and "leopards" and all the destructive elements that inhabit our interior psyche as well as the world around us. As Christians, we know that true freedom can come only through a prayerful attentiveness to our "hearts," where Jesus is to become completely our Lord, Savior and spouse.

Coming down from the heights of our own controlled self-image and pride, we must have the courage to enter into the process of *metanoia*, the conversion or return to our true self, which cannot be realized except in our oneness with Christ. This means to look honestly at our creatureliness, our existential "nothingness." This nothingness is beyond our rational control to understand. Understanding is a gift which the Fathers of the desert called *penthos*, an abiding sense of our inner, creaturely poverty before the rich lovingness of God. This is given to the *anawim*, the *remnant* of God's poor ones in spirit who dare to confront their non-being, their state of nothingness before God's *allness*.

You Ravish My Heart

> You ravish my heart,
> my sister, my promised bride,
> you ravish my heart
> with a single one of your glances,
> with one single pearl of your necklace.
> What spells lie in your love,
> my sister, my promised bride!
> How delicious is your love, more delicious than wine:
> How fragrant your perfumes,
> more fragrant than all other spices!
> Your lips, my promised one,
> distill wild honey.
> Honey and milk
> are under your tongue;
> and the scent of your garments
> is like the scent of Lebanon.
> She is a garden enclosed,

my sister, my promised bride;
a garden enclosed,
a sealed fountain.
Your shoots form an orchard of pomegranate trees,
the rarest essences are yours:
nard and saffron,
calamus and cinnamon,
with all the incense-bearing trees;
myrrh and aloes,
with the subtlest odors.
Fountain that makes the gardens fertile,
well of living water,
streams flowing down from Lebanon (4:9-15).

1.   The bride responds to the plea of the groom that she descend from her high places, so filled with destructive forces, and come to him. This humble "coming," with full haste and courage to pass beyond the "animals" that threaten her safety, pleases the groom. He begins ecstatically again to praise her beauty, which becomes more ravishing of his heart as she responds more heroically to allow him to have complete control in her life.

2.   He calls her "my sister, my promised bride." By taking upon himself our humanity, Jesus becomes brother to all men and women and we become his brothers and sisters, who have as our creator the one heavenly Father. But Jesus can call us his sister in a different way: "And stretching out his hand towards his disciples he said, 'Here are my mother and my brothers. Anyone who does the will of my Father in heaven, he is my brother and sister and mother!'" (Mt 12:49-50).

By his incarnation, death and resurrection and through the outpouring of his Spirit, Jesus Christ makes it possible for us, his followers, to be "regenerated" or reborn into a new life, whereby we share Christ's very own divine life. We are lifted up by a rebirth in the Spirit to be participators in God's very own nature (2 Pt 1:4).

"I tell you most solemnly,
unless a man is born through water and the Spirit,
he cannot enter the kingdom of God:

what is born of the flesh is flesh;
what is born of the Spirit is spirit" (Jn 3:5-6).

"The Spirit himself and our spirit bear united witness that we are
children of God. And if we are children we are heirs as well: heirs
of God and coheirs with Christ, sharing his sufferings so as to
share his glory" (Rom 8:16-17). Jesus through his Spirit makes
it possible for us to enter into a divinization process whereby we
as fully human beings share in his divinity as his humanity shared
in his eternal divine life—we, however, by grace, he by his very
own nature as God from all eternity. Yet the good news is that
we are of the same stock, not only as human beings, but also as
sharers in his divine life by grace:

> For the one who sanctifies, and the ones who are sanc-
> tified, are of the same stock; that is why he openly
> calls them brothers in the text: I shall announce your
> name to my brothers, praise you in full assembly; or
> the text: In him I hope; or the text: Here I am with
> the children whom God has given me (Heb 2:11-13)

There can be no true nuptial union except among equals
where each partner in the marriage gives to the other the complete gift of self, but also receives the gift of the other. The good
news that Jesus makes possible is that you and I and all his
disciples are, by his Spirit in baptism, lifted up to enter into the
royalty of God our king. We become, not commoners who are
somehow or other accepted by the king's prince as his bride, but
we are literally born again into the very family of God. We are
a royal princess capable of wedding the crowned prince, Christ.
Our God-given beauty ravishes him.

3.   Christ, who belongs to us individually as our spouse through
betrothal, says that one single glance, or one single pearl of our
necklace, ravishes his heart. The bride has only one eye, for him,
and this fidelity and devotion ravish him. Sufferings have not
turned the bride from the groom but have made her adhere more
passionately to him, and this devotion thrills him. How delighted
we are when we understand the humility of God, made manifest
to us through Jesus Christ and recognized by the Spirit of love!

He is not only pleased when we adhere to him in all the prunings he brings about in our lives; such fidelity actually thrills him. And so he is drawn even more to give himself to us individually in total oneness.

The Spell of Love

1.   What a mystery for "little ones" that God truly seeks our return of love after he has first loved us! God is truly God, not because of his infinite power over "all the other gods" or created forces, but because of his condescending love that humbly awaits our return of love. God in Christ is truly a spouse who passionately, even unto the death on the cross, desires our love in response to his complete and perfect love for each of us individually. Truly Jesus acts out what Yahweh speaks through the lips of Jeremiah the prophet:

> "I have loved you with an everlasting love,
> so I am constant in my affection for you" (Jer 31:3).

The reason why Christ ardently desires your love is that it is the love of God himself that abounds in your heart through the Spirit who is given to us (Rom 5:5).

> My dear people,
> let us love one another since love comes from God
> and everyone who loves is begotten by God and knows
>   God (1 Jn 4:7).

This love was imparted to your heart in your new birth in baptism. This is why Christ, the groom, can say to you: "What spells lie in your love!"

2.   He again calls you his sister, his promised bride. Jesus is always the Way leading you to the Father of both himself and yourself. They bring you home to your true family that shares with Jesus, your brother, the very trinitarian life of Father, Son and Holy Spirit. But the awesome mystery is that Jesus loves you also passionately, more than any bridegroom loves his bride. You are truly his "promised bride." That phrase from the lips of Christ must fill you with strength and consolation when you are caught

in the darkness of temptations and trials or in discouragement at seeing your own failures to respond to the dignity to which God has called you.

The Delirium of Love

1.   The groom, appealing to sense experiences, likens the bride's love[26] to wine, but he says it is even more delicious. In 1:2 the bride says of the groom's love for her that her "love is more delightful than wine." Now the groom says that the love of the bride for him is more delicious than wine. It implies a greater degree of intimacy, of intoxication, now that the bride has entered into the betrothal with her beloved. This spell-casting power of the bride's love for her spouse is beautifully captured by St. John of the Cross:

> The power and the tenacity of love is great, for love captures and binds God himself. Happy is the loving soul, since she possesses God for her prisoner, and He is surrendered to all her desires. God is such that those who act with love and friendship toward Him will make Him do all they desire, but if they act otherwise there is no speaking to him nor power with Him even though they go to extremes. Yet by love they bind Him with one hair.[27]

2.   The bride's perfumes are more fragrant than all other spices. Solomon is reputed to have had the best ointments obtainable. But here is the "greater than Solomon" saying the fragrance of the perfumes of his bride is superior to all other spices. One reason is that Christ has given his bride the perfumes made out of his myrrh, human sufferings unto death, and frankincense, his divine royalty. But she also has added to the fragrance her own sufferings through the purifications undergone to surrender herself completely to the love of her spouse.

3.   It is not merely lips that meet in a kiss of love, but two persons embrace; their lips touch as a sign of sweet surrender to each other. The groom calls her his "promised" one. He is totally espoused to her and yet he has not consummated his love with her. He touches her lips and utters his happiness that those lips

bring a sweetness to him: "Your lips distill wild honey." Anyone who has fallen in love understands what the groom is saying with this phrase. Two in love constantly resort to *honey* as a phrase of endearment, for they have found kisses as sweet as honey. Union is what God calls us to, both with him and with our neighbor. To move toward such oneness is always a "sweet," like honey, experience.

4. "Honey and milk are under your tongue," says the groom. He praises his bride for her conversation. Out of the love for him she has experienced she speaks words that are sweet and nourishing to others who hear her. The tongue fashions the words physically, but it is the "heart" out of which flow the honey and milk of love and kindness toward others. Such nourishing love is clothed in words. Words betray the reality of true love, or the selfishness of the speaker. St. James writes:

> We use it (the tongue) to bless the Lord and Father, but we also use it to curse men who are made in God's image: the blessing and the curse come out of the same mouth. My brothers, this must be wrong—does any water supply give a flow of fresh water and salt water out of the pipe? Can a fig tree give you olives, my brothers, or a vine give figs? No more can sea water give you fresh water (Jas 3:9-12).

The true test of our oneness with Christ and our experience of how much he loves us is how we think and converse with other human beings. Just as it is impossible for a good fruit tree to bring forth bad fruit, so it is impossible for a Christian, who truly experiences his or her inner beauty, to utter words filled with honey and milk to nourish some and with only vinegar for others. We pray and seek at all times to live out our prayer-experience in the words of David:

> May the words of my mouth always find favor,
> and the whispering of my heart,
> in your presence, Yahweh,
> my Rock, my Redeemer! (Ps 19:14).

5. "The scent of your garments is like the scent of Lebanon."

Animals and human beings who live close to nature can pick up body scents from garments. The bride presents herself to others out of her interior oneness with her beloved who has called her into being beautiful in all her relationships. The smell of her garments gives off a smell of the incorruptible cedar wood of Lebanon. The bride gives off a fragrance from her external actions that covers her inner life and flows out of her union with the king unto life eternal.

Christ calls us all to spread a sweet smell everywhere that will lead others to a share of immortal life. This is the same image St. Paul uses as he exhorts the early Christians:

> Thanks be to God who, wherever he goes, makes us, in Christ, partners of his triumph, and through us is spreading the knowledge of himself, like a sweet smell, everywhere. We are Christ's incense to God for those who are being saved and for those who are not; for the last, the smell of life that leads to life. And who could be qualified for work like this?... In Christ, we speak as men of sincerity, as envoys of God and in God's presence (2 Cor 2:14-17).

An Enclosed Garden

1. How often in scripture we find God relating to human beings in a garden setting. He made man and woman according to his own image and placed them in a garden in Eden (Gn 2:8). It is the place where God brings forth abundant new life, plants and animals. But, above all, it is in this garden where God meets his beloved children in person-to-person communication. Unfortunately, it is also in the garden that Adam and Eve sin and break down the inner communication with God. Jesus often prayed in the Garden of Gethsemane, where his prayer was to undo the failure of the first human being to surrender himself in prayer to God. In his interior battle, Jesus cried out: "My soul is sorrowful to the point of death" (Mk 14:34). It was in the garden of Joseph of Arimathea that Jesus was buried after his death on the cross, and in that garden he first appears as risen to give that life to the repentant sinner, Mary Magdalen. A garden is a symbol of the

future transformation of the entire world through the Lamb of God (Rv 22:1-2).

The groom looks at his bride and, as almost thinking aloud, he reflects how she has become a garden enclosed, she who is his sister, his promised bride. She has been surrounded by his protective love as by a high wall that keeps out the little foxes, the lions and leopards, and all other forces that would destroy her belonging entirely to him. The enclosed garden is a beautiful symbol of the bride who is being called into the mystical union with her beloved, Christ. Nothing outside can attract her now. And within the enclosure she is about to experience her oneness with Christ, being transformed into him so she loses all sense of a separated selfhood, different from her groom. He and she will become one in this garden enclosed, in her "heart," where their union can never be broken or destroyed.

2. She is a sealed fountain, a fountain that bubbles up with fresh, life-giving water from deep down, but is covered over and all around from contamination from any outside force. She is a fountain, but a fountain is nothing other than the water that flows out from it. She has drunk of Christ, the living water, and has become a fountain of that living water to others.

> "Whoever drinks this water
> Will get thirsty again;
> but anyone who drinks the water that I shall give
> will never be thirsty again:
> the water that I shall give
> will turn into a spring inside him, welling up to
> eternal life" (Jn 4:13-14).

3. The groom seeks to describe the fertility that will come when he and she consummate their union. She is a fruit-bearing garden that, like Eden, produces first an orchard of pomegranate trees. The pomegranate is a fruit often found in Jewish symbolism to indicate Israel's worship. The hem of the priest's garment was adorned with embroidered pomegranates. The pillars that held up the Temple had such fruit sculptured around them (1Kgs 7:18-20). The bride is beautiful and fruitful due to her worship

of her Lord. And Christ's devotion to her is caught in the symbol of the pomegranate as well: the white seeds immersed in crimson juice, the cost of his love for her and the world by his death on the cross. The bride brings forth the pomegranate fruit and also is nourished by the fruit, for it is the love of her groom, dying for her on the cross, that begets her into new life. She remembers and contemplates ceaselessly the words of the prophet Zechariah: "And if anyone asks him, 'Then what are these wounds on your body?' he will reply, 'These I received in the house of my friends'" (Zec 13:6).

4.   The bride is a fertile garden that brings forth other fruits, rare spices of exquisite fragrances. The seed has fallen into the earth and now produces a hundredfold. Such exotic fruits come from the garden that has become fruitful by the power of the risen Lord, her spouse. Whatever be the virtues and fruits she brings forth, she knows she is only the earth, but he is the seed that has fallen into the earth. The fruit of a good life, of virtues that give forth heavenly fragrances to all passers-by, comes both from the earth and from the seed that buries itself in death in the earth. She is humbly aware as Christ praises his bride that all is his gift: "And there is no limit to the blessings which God can send you—he will make sure that you will always have all you need for yourselves in every possible circumstance, and still have something to spare for all sorts of good works" (2 Cor 9:9).

5.   The bride is again compared by the groom to a fountain, but this time he praises his beloved because she brings living water to make the gardens fertile. She is a fruitful garden insofar as she allows the seed, Christ, to come and take root in her earth—and so are all other Christians called to be fruitful gardens. Yet the bride is praised because she brings Christ, the only water that yields eternal life, to make other persons fruitful:

> He is like a tree that is planted
> by water streams,
> yielding its fruit in season (Ps 1:3).

Christ is the living water (Jn 4:10), but in his humility he has need of disciples to be "streams" flowing down from "Lebanon," a symbol of Christ's transcendent divinity. Such streams bring the life-giving waters of Christ's Spirit to others, who in their gardens bring forth fruit in great abundance. The bride is one of those who become wells of this living water—a fountain that makes other gardens fertile. To what dignity Christ calls you, his bride, to be the channel of his life-giving graces to the many you are privileged to be sent to serve!

Come, Holy Spirit

The Bride:

> Awake, north wind,
> come, wind of the south!
> Breathe over my garden,
> to spread its sweet smell around.
> Let my Beloved come into his garden,
> let him taste its rarest fruits (4:16).

1. The bride has matured very much in her love for her spouse. Before, she did not understand the dynamic process of seeming death unto resurrection, of her need to suffer whatever was needed to break down her ego in order to obtain eternal life in the deepest union with Christ. She prayed that the cup of suffering be taken away from her. Now, so filled with ardent desire to possess Christ more intimately than ever, she prays that the Holy Spirit, the wind that stirs all life into being, should come upon her, the garden. The Spirit is first called the "north wind," which brings the conditions of winter. The Spirit blows a cold wind that dries up and withers the flowers and plants. It freezes the ground and covers the earth with a blanket of seeming death and stillness. Yet the bride knows that such tribulations brought about by the Spirit of God's love are preparing for a greater harvest. What seems to be dryness, cold, no life, is only dormant for a while. In such seeming sterility and deathly stillness, the bride knows life is beginning to stir. The winter wheat lies in the cold earth, beneath much snow, but it is preparing itself for the harvest.

     She has learned through her past sufferings, as Job did, that

God is testing her for new riches. Stripped of all his earthly posses-
sions, of his children and even his wife's affections, Job sat on
the dung heap, confessing:

> This I know: that my Avenger lives,
> and he, the Last, will take his stand on earth.
> After my awaking, he will set me close to him,
> and from my flesh I shall look on God (Jb 19:25-26).

Job experienced what the bride had already undergone: "Let him
test me in the crucible: I shall come out pure gold" (Jb 23:10).
All the saints in the Christian church have understood the necessity
of suffering with Christ in order to enter into glory with him (Rom
8:17). They knew that without the sufferings necessary to relin-
quish control over their own lives, over God and over the lives
of others, there would be no sharing with their risen Lord, Jesus.
And so the bride cries out to wake up the Holy Spirit—the "north
wind," the purifying love of the risen Jesus—to hurry and do its
important work. She is now ready for everything, provided only
the sufferings will bring her to the mystical marriage with her
spouse.

2.   She calls on the Holy Spirit to come as the "wind of the
south." This is a warm, spring breeze that brings forth rains and
makes seeds soften and plants germinate, fruit trees to blossom
and flowers to send forth their fragrance in flaming colors of new
life. The bride is burning with desire that Christ bring forth new
life within her. She knows that only the Holy Spirit can pour out
more of the love of God that already abounds in her heart (Rom
5:5), so she begs for his coming to bring her into greater oneness
with her beloved.

3.   She begs that the Holy Spirit breathe his breath of love over
her garden to spread its sweet smell around. St. John of the Cross
notes the difference between God's breathing in the soul and his
breathing through the soul as through a garden:

> To breathe in the soul is to infuse graces, gifts and vir-
> tues. To breathe through the soul is to touch and put
> in motion the virtues and perfections already given,
> renewing and moving them in such a way that they

of themselves afford the soul wonderful fragrance and
sweetness as when you shake aromatic spices and they
spread their abundant fragrance which prior to this
was neither so strong nor so highly perceptible.[28]

4.   The bride now invites her beloved to come into what is
really *his* garden to taste its rarest fruits. She is professing that
all her virtues and inner beauty and loveliness come completely
from Christ. She belongs to him; she is his garden, for all her life
has come from him: "...for cut off from me you can do nothing"
(Jn 15:5). Everything she possesses or can do, all she existentially
is comes to her from the Father through the Son in his Spirit of
love: "Everything that is perfect, which is given us from above;
it comes down from the Father of all light" (Jas 1:17).

   She is offering herself in the deepest, most personal part of
her being to her groom as the rarest of fruits. She begs him to
taste it, eat it and enjoy the gift she wishes to make of herself.

   She wishes to hold back nothing.

Chapter Five

The Bridegroom:

> I come into my garden,
> my sister, my promised bride,
> I gather my myrrh and balsam,
> I eat my honey and my honeycomb,
> I drink my wine and my milk.
> Eat, friends, and drink,
> drink deep, my dearest friends (5:1).

His Garden

1.   The groom accepts the invitation of the bride and enters into
the garden that is the bride, but he claims it as *his* garden, for
he recognizes what she said as true, that all her beauty and all
her virtues and gifts have come from him, the Christ. But he also
affirms that he accepts the offer of the gift of herself and does
her honor by calling her his garden. For he has espoused himself
to her and she to him. What is hers is now his by a free-will gift

of the bride. Can we in this life ever understand what joy it must give to Christ when we surrender and give back to him what has always been his by creation but is now recognized in a new way by him through transformation as a free gift from his bride? He first loves us, and in his Spirit he empowers us to surrender ourselves in return for all we have received from him.

2.   Again the groom calls his bride his sister, his promised bride. Sister is placed before bride to indicate that the individual Christian is first a sister of Christ in the new birth through baptism that brings her into the divine family and makes her a co-heir of heaven with Christ forever. Her becoming a bride of Christ can follow only upon her first being lifted up by what Christ has done:

> But God loved us with so much love that he was generous with his mercy: when we were dead through our sins, he brought us to life with Christ—it is through grace that you have been saved—and raised us up with him and gave us a place with him in heaven, in Christ Jesus (Eph 2:4-6).

3.   The spouse accepts the invitation of the bride and does four things: He comes into the garden he calls his own. He gathers myrrh and balsam. He eats his honey and honeycomb. He drinks his wine and milk. We should note that Christ is coming to claim his bride in nuptial union, and so he partakes of all that is of the bride, all that she has brought forth in her garden, in her interior life, and claims it as his very own. He first gathers his myrrh and balsam. Before the bride could embrace humility and sufferings and bring forth a life of virtues as spices, she had to receive as seeds the myrrh and balsam from the life of Christ. Myrrh was presented to the babe in the stable at Bethlehem by the three Wise Men, to indicate both the condescension of the Son of God in taking upon himself the form of man, yes, even the form of a weak, suffering child, and the sufferings he would bear for us human beings in order that we might be healed by his great love for us. The bride has learned humility and sufferings by confronting the dark areas in her life and enduring the various nights of purification in her desire to become worthy of her bridegroom. Now the groom rejoices as he accepts the "myrrh" and "balsam" that have made him so ardently desire to possess the bride completely.

Love is Like Honey

4. He eats of his honey and honeycomb. He had earlier noted that her lips distill wild honey. Here he eats of her kisses and sees how sweet is her love for Him:

> "If only my people would listen...
> I would feed you on pure wheat
> and satisfy you with the wild rock honey"
> (Ps 81:13,16).

Christ feeds all who come to him with the bread of life, his very own body. He feeds us with the wild honey that is found in the desert. This is his intimate love for those who enter into the richness and sweetness of his infinite love for them. And now he is gathering from the bride some of that transformed, sweet love, that first came from him; but in an exciting way he finds it as new honey, the unique love of the bride for him.

5. He drinks his wine and his milk. Wine indicates joy and intoxication coming from the celebration at a banquet. At the Last Supper Jesus poured out his abundant love for mankind in the form of joy-inducing wine. His heart overflowed with joy as he was about to pour himself out on our behalf: "I have longed to eat this passover with you before I suffer because I tell you, I shall not eat it again until it is fulfilled in the kingdom of God...I shall not drink wine until the kingdom of God comes" (Lk 22:15-18). And now he enters into the garden of the heart of his bride and drinks of the wine of her great love for him. He tells her he has come to drink his wine, to receive her love for him that has been produced because she has deeply drunk of his intoxicating love.

He drinks milk, a symbol of gentleness, food which nourishes babies and is easily digested. The bride has drunk of the gentleness of Christ, which has weaned her away from false doctrines and prepared her for the intoxication of his intimate love for her. Now he drinks of this gentleness, this mothering of his bride of the Christ-life in her, and it thrills him to feed on her love since he first gave her to drink of his love.

Come to the Wedding Banquet

6.   Now the groom turns to his friends, those invited to the wedding banquet, and invites them to eat and drink deeply. He calls them his dearest friends. They like the bride are invited to partake of the food and drink so abundantly laid out. This recalls God's invitation to the *anawim* to come to the banquet and be fed abundantly with God's love, provided only they bring a thirst and appetite for the food and drink that God will furnish. It cannot be purchased; it is freely given by God as Isaiah describes it:

> Oh, come to the water all you who are thirsty;
> though you have no money, come!
> Buy corn without money, and eat,
> and, at no cost, wine and milk.
> Why spend money on what is not bread,
> your wages on what fails to satisfy?
> Listen, listen to me, and you will have good things
>   to eat
> and rich food to enjoy.
> Pay attention, come to me;
> listen, and your soul will live (Is 55:1-3).

God truly wishes all to eat and drink deeply of his infinite love. But, alas, how few Christians seek ardently and perseveringly, as this bride has done, to move beyond desiring only the things of this world that cannot satisfy the burning longing God has placed in all human hearts to possess God's everlasting love! "You prepare a table before me..." (Ps 23:5). In the Eastern Christian churches, the priest often during the Liturgy and especially at the beginning and end kisses the altar, the table that God has prepared for us. For this table is Christ around whom we are invited to gather and receive of God's outpouring love under the species of bread and wine. No money is needed. We are asked to approach with faith, love and the fear of the Lord and we will have our fill. There is no scarcity of this food and drink. It is unending in its supply and in its power to nourish and intoxicate us with the joy of the Holy Spirit.

He calls us his dearest friends:

> "You are my friends,
> if you do what I command you...
> I call you friends, because I have made known to you
>   everything
> I have learnt from my Father" (Jn 15:14-15).

The good news that Jesus has come to bring us through his Spirit is that we can all be called into nuptial union with him if only we are ready to surrender to his wishes as the bride has done.

Fourth Poem

(5:2-6:3)

The Bride:

> I sleep, but my heart is awake.
> I hear my Beloved knocking.
> "Open to me, my sister, my love,
> my dove, my perfect one,
> for my head is covered with dew,
> my locks with the drops of night."
>
> —"I have taken off my tunic,
> am I to put it on again?
> I have washed my feet,
> am I to dirty them again?"
>
> My Beloved thrust his hand
> through the hole in the door;
> I trembled to the core of my being.
> Then I rose
> to open to my Beloved,
> myrrh ran off my hands,
> pure myrrh off my fingers,
> on to the handle of the bolt (5:2-5).

1. The bride seems to be reflecting to herself that even when she is sleeping her heart is awake listening for the voice of her beloved. One manner in which we can understand this is given to us by those well advanced in contemplative prayer. The presence of Jesus Christ through faith becomes so strong and penetrates so deeply into the very unconscious of the contemplative that even in sleep Christ is communing with the individual who seems to respond in faith, hope and love through

93

the inner operations of the Holy Spirit. In the Russian classic on the Jesus Prayer, the Pilgrim writes:

> After having spent some five months in solitude and prayer which filled me with sweet sensations, I grew so used to it that I practiced it constantly. In the end I felt that it was going on by itself in my mind and heart, not only while I was awake but also in my sleep. It never ceased for a single moment in whatever business I might have been doing. My soul gave thanks to God, and my heart melted away in continuous joy.[29]

It is possible for the contemplative, the bride of Christ, to become so centered in the heart with the presence of the indwelling Christ that the thought and presence of him are always somewhere close to waking consciousness, even in sleep. Christ is operating, even in sleep, in dreams and in delicate movements of the heart, so that it can be said that such a contemplative never loses awareness of his presence, never stops "listening" to his voice.

This phrase also could refer to a change in the bride in regard to her awareness of the things of the world around her as a result of the new, heightened awareness of the all-ness of Christ, her beloved. As the controlled self moves more and more away from self-centeredness and an ego-consciousness to a Christ-consciousness, the things in the material world take on, as far as importance goes, a sleep-like quality in one's awareness. The world and its multiplicity are there, but in a way they are not there. The focus of attention resembles a sleep, while the *heart*, the inner core of deeper consciousness, penetrated by the Spirit's faith, hope and love, is inwardly awake and filled with a oneness in Christ.

Knocking at the Door

2. The bride hears her beloved knocking on the door. It is as the author of the Book of Revelation depicts Christ: "Look, I am standing at the door, knocking. If one of you hears me calling and opens the door, I will come in to share his meal, side by side with him" (Rv 3:20). We believe that the indwelling Christ is

always within us. But there are special moments when, if we are attentive, he seems to offer us a grace whereby we "awake" to his inbreaking love and hear his overtures to enter into more intimate communion with him. These are the precious moments you have surely experienced often in your love-relationship with Christ over years of growing in oneness with him. When such moments come to you, you hear Christ fill you with consolation and a sense of your inner beauty, which convinces you he truly wants your love. And so the groom asks his sister, his love, his dove, his perfect one to open up to his presence, for he wishes to enter into a deeper oneness with her.

3.   He complains that his head is covered with dew and his hair with the drops of night. *Dew* in Scripture is often a symbol of God's blessings, usually tied to eternal life and associated with the Holy Spirit who softly and gently, like dew, falls upon those who have been purified with divine life.

The night that covers the hair of the groom perhaps is best reflected in St. Paul's use of that phrase when he wrote: "The night is almost over, it will be daylight soon—let us give up all the things we prefer to do under cover of the dark; let us arm ouselves and appear in the light" (Rom 13:12-13). Christ is the light, but he humbly enters into our darkness. Yet in so many ways we do not comprehend that he who has become "a worm and no man" for our sakes is, nevertheless, God. He wishes to dispel from our hearts all darkness, all signs of the night of sin and death, with his resurrectional presence of warming light, if only we open the door of our hearts to his light that dispels all night.

What Do You Want Me to Do?

1.   The bride answers the petition of the groom that he be allowed to enter. She says that she has already taken off her tunic. Does he want her to put it on again? She has already washed her feet. Does he want her to dirty them again? Many commentators on this passage interpret the actions of the bride as a bit selfish. The groom asks her to open the door and she is comfortably lying in bed. She does not want to make the effort to get out of bed, dress and open the door. But the bride has accepted the life of hardships and has successfully endured them so as to be purified

and already espoused to her beloved. To all who seriously seek greater union with Christ there comes a period of conflict arranged by the divine physician. He asks his bride in a way to suffer what seems to be a return to a lower level. The contemplative hesitates to accept the conflict, not so much out of a lack of generosity but rather out of a realization of the great union and love she has already attained with Christ.

Toward the relinquishing of the last vestiges of self-control before one enters into the mystical marriage, Christ calls the soul to open up the areas within its very own unconscious. What seems to rush out are oceans of humiliating defects which Christ's bride had felt were long ago conquered and transformed. Fits of temper, harsh words, angry moods, petty criticisms of others, jealousies and envy riddle the heart. It is a night that seems very dense and dark. A sense comes over the individual that, although Christ is present knocking, yet she seems so sinful, so wretched and humiliated by her state of weakness, worldliness and even a sense that she has seemingly wilfully turned away from her beloved.

You are convinced that you haven't even begun in the way of perfection. You find yourself reprimanding others. Your hard heart seems to despise everyone. Your mind cannot concentrate on any given topic, especially on anything spiritual. You find it difficult to recall anything. You stand immobilized as before a steel wall of blackness. Are you losing your mind? You have no control over it. Are you heading for a complete mental breakdown? Blasphemies against the name of God rise up. Lewd, sexual pictures and desires stir up from within you. You have absurd suspicions about others around you, even about God that he has left you and despises you. You feel as though you are slipping out of reality and you cannot grasp anything solid to hold on to.

St. John of the Cross describes what is happening and gives the reason for it:

> God divests the faculties, affections and senses, both spiritual and sensory, interior and exterior. He leaves the intellect in darkness, the will in aridity, the memory in emptiness and the affections in supreme affliction,

bitterness and anguish, by depriving the soul of the feeling and satisfaction it previously obtained from spiritual blessings. For this privation is one of the conditions required that the spiritual form, which is the union of love, may be introduced in the spirit and united with it. The Lord works all of this in the soul by means of a pure and dark contemplation...[30]

The Beloved at the Door

1. Evidently the beloved is not displeased with the bride's hesitation. He sees that she is merely wondering humbly why she has gone backward in her love for him? He thrusts his hand through the hole in the door. Yet he is unable to open the door for the bride has the key. How Christ patiently waits for us to rise up and to allow him to come into our lives and to bring to us whatever sufferings he wishes for us in order that we can completely abandon ourselves to him and be completely purified of all creaturely attachments!

2. The bride trembles to the core of her being at the close presence of her beloved. She also trembles at her own weakness and what seems too great for her to suffer. We find ourselves on the threshold of a breakthrough in our intimacy with God, and it is a frightening experience. Isaiah trembled before the throne of the Almighty as he saw the six-winged seraphs covering their faces and their feet with their wings (Is 6:2). Moses bowed down in reverence and holy fear as God passed him by on the mountain (Ex 34:8). When we have those moments of deep encounter with God as the Holy One, the almighty, the source of all being, we are blessed with the experience of the bride who "trembled" to the core of her being.

But we can also tremble before what we think God is asking us to suffer in order to have a part with his son. Jesus trembled, shook with fear, sweated blood as he agonized in the garden before what he saw the heavenly Father asking him to suffer on our behalf: "In his anguish he prayed even more earnestly, and his sweat fell to the ground like great drops of blood" (Lk 22:44). At times, how great the cost to have a part with Christ! We may have already given up so much. But, God, how can you ask this?

I will willingly bear everything, go anywhere for love of you; but how can I undergo this agony? How can I endure this living hell? I cannot do it. I tremble with fear! O, God, come to my rescue; O, Lord, make haste to help me!

3.   Then we find the bride rising to open the door to her beloved. She repents her fears and worries of how things are to come about. She is resolved to do whatever the groom asks of her by way of abandoning herself entirely to his will. He can do whatever he wishes with her. But to arrive at this new act of self-sacrifice and surrender, she is reminded what she must do by the myrrh that drops out of her hands and bathes her fingers with choicest fragrance. Myrrh is a symbol of humility that comes through mortification and death to doing one's own will in order to embrace completely the will of God. Myrrh is sweet to the smell, one of the most expensive of fragrances; but it is very bitter to the taste. It stands for the fragrance of holiness that comes in the joy of sharing intimately with the eternal life of her beloved, Christ. But it also suggests the bitterness of the death necessary to attain eternal life.

He Is Gone!

> I opened to my Beloved,
> but he had turned his back and gone!
> My soul failed at his flight.
> I sought him but I did not find him,
> I called to him but he did not answer.
> The watchmen came upon me
> as they made their rounds in the City
> They beat me, they wounded me,
> they took away my cloak,
> they who guard the ramparts (5:6-7).

1.   She opens the door so her beloved may enter but, alas, he has turned his back and gone! She had struggled with the dark night of whether she would give him total direction in her life. She came out of the inner hell that tortured her with the vivid expectantcy of embracing her beloved, only to find him gone. What a beautiful phrase it is that expresses the new level of abandonment she makes in her mind to her beloved! "I opened to my Beloved." She is ready to give herself totally to him, to give whatever he may ask of her. She wants to consummate her burning love for him with complete self-surrender. Yet he is not ready to take her gift. The divine physician knows that to make such an act of abandonment in one's will is not quite the same as to fulfull such a state as an habitual attitude at all times in one's daily life.

2.   Her "soul failed" her at his flight. Just as she had resolved with burning passion and interior suffering to bear all things her beloved would ask of her, she opens the door to find that he has fled away. Can we ever comprehend the love strategy of our beloved? We recall the triad that the father of Christian mysticism, St. Gregory of Nyssa of the 4th Century, worked out to describe the ebb and flow of the mystical path. From light, consolation and loving union with Christ, the contemplative is hurled into a level of shadow. Aridity, trials and temptations begin to rise up. He stands nearby but is not immediately perceived and experienced. Then the fearful night of total darkness engulfs the soul. Here the bride expresses her agony, as her soul fails her. In spiral fashion the triad of light, shadow and darkness repeats itself again and again, always in greater intensity.

Lovers often resort to certain ploys to intensify the desire, the pursuit of the other, which makes the union all the more intense and all-consuming. Christ in his infinite wisdom has his own love games to play with us. He touches us with his consoling presence and our hearts melt like molten wax as we seemingly merge into a new-found oneness that we feel will never be shattered. Then he plunges us into absence as he mysteriously withdraws. He is molding us into the person he has always seen us to be in his Father's eternal love for us. He burns out of our hearts all vestiges of self-control. Who can ever say what is more important: to be in ecstatic union with him, or to be entering into the shadows of his nebulous presence, or to be drowning in the darkness of his complete absence, at least in our feeling?

The mystical doctor, St. John of the Cross, evidently writing out of his own experiences of the workings of the divine spouse in the contemplative's soul, phrases the importance of such purifications which alone can prepare one for even greater and purer union with him.

> O sweet cautery,
> O delightful wound!
> O gentle hand! O delicate touch
> That tastes of eternal life
> And pays every debt!
> In killing You changed death to life.[31]

I Sought Him

1.   The bride not finding her spouse outside at the door when she opened it for him to enter, rushes out to seek him, but ends up bitterly saying: "...but I did not find him, I called to him but he did not answer." The pain of absence of a loved one can only be understood by one who has experienced the joys of intimacy. When the beloved leaves, it is similar to having oneself cut into two parts. The disorientation, the fragmentation that is caused in the soul of the bride stirs within her the passionate desire to seek him whom she so ardently loves. Added to the reality of being separated from her beloved is the pain that perhaps she was not quick enough to have responded to his call when he knocked. She is bitter with sorrow and confusion, wondering whether she was the cause of his withdrawal from her. Will she ever find him again? What can she do to make amends? The words of Christ, the beloved, on the cross express what she suffers on a spiritual plane:

> I am like water draining away,
> my bones are all disjointed,
> my heart is like wax,
> melting inside me;
> my palate is drier that a potsherd
> and my tongue is stuck to my jaw (Ps 22:14).

The bride finds pleasure in nothing. Her heart is emptied. Here is operating a purifying love that the groom wishes for her. It will dry up her desire for any creature or person, as she with burning love seeks to find him.

The Watchmen Beat Her

1. Overcome with inner grief and deep distrust of herself for possibly having been the cause of her beloved's flight from her, she goes into the city calling for him. The watchmen of the city come upon her in a condition of dishevelment and think she is mad to be running about the city at night. She had earlier (3:3) sought her beloved in the city and had asked help from the watchmen. But now their reaction is outright aggression. They beat her, wound her and take away her cloak. They attack her as though she is an enemy to the city, "they who guard the ramparts."

The watchmen can symbolize any force of the world that should be a help to find Christ, but in reality turns out to be destructive of any union with him. For the contemplative soul the watchmen could be church teachers who by their special role within the church are given to protect the citadel of the church from heretical attacks of the enemies of darkness. The contemplative advances toward the mystical marriage and comes to learn to distrust her own judgment in her case. "What is illusion and what is reality?" she asks as she loses control over her "self." In the period between moving away from any objective control through her rational consciousness and reaching a new oneness as a permanent state of union with Christ, she flounders in the dark night.

She seeks advice from the "watchmen," those who should by their office be able to help her find her spouse. But they attack her. Jesus had promised his followers that they would have to suffer persecution, and some would even be put to death for his sake. They should rejoice when this happens to them: "Happy are you when people abuse you and persecute you and speak all kinds of calumny against you on my account. Rejoice and be glad, for your reward will be great in heaven; this is how they persecuted the prophets before you" (Mt 5:11-12).

Great Christian mystics of all ages have discovered that part of the dark night purification in their movement to greater union with Christ was to come from friends and church leaders. Mystics were often suspected of being demented. St. John of the Cross was literally beaten by his own fellow religious and thrown into prison for months where he was heaped with insults. St. Teresa of Avila understood what agonies she suffered from well-intended spiritual directors who suspected her of being hysterical and on the verge of madness. Friends even abandon us as Job found his friends, his very own wife and children doing to him.

How exactly this suffering is described by the psalmist:

> I shudder at the enemy's shouts,
>   at the howling of the wicked;
> they bring misery crashing down on me,
>   and vent their fury on me.
>
> My heart aches in my breast,
> Death's terrors assail me,
> fear and trembling descend on me,
>   horror overwhelms me.
>
> And I say,
> "Oh for the wings of a dove
>   to fly away and find rest."
> How far I would take my flight,
>   and make a new home in the desert!
>
> There I should soon find shelter
>   from the raging wind,
> and from the tempest, Lord, that destroys,
>   and from their malicious tongues.
>
> I can see how Violence
>   and Discord fill the city;
> day and night they stalk together
>   along the city walls.
>
> Sorrow and Misery live inside,
>   Ruin is an inmate;
> Tyranny and Treachery are never absent
>   from its central square.
>
> Were it an enemy who insulted me,
>   I could put up with that;

had a rival got the better of me,
  I could hide from him.

But you, a man of my own rank,
  a colleague and a friend,
to whom sweet conversation bound me
  in the house of God! (Ps 55:3-14).

2. The watchmen took away her cloak. This could mean they removed from her the sign of some protective covering that was meant to keep her secured and protected from adverse elements. Now she is stripped even of the "safe" counsels of her church authorities. She is "abroad" without any defenses or protections. She seemingly has no one to help her, to come to her rescue.

I Am Sick With Love

I charge you,
daughters of Jerusalem,
if you should find my Beloved,
What must you tell him...?
That I am sick with love (5:8).

1. True love always focuses attention away from oneself onto the beloved. The bride can receive no help from teachers about the intricate ways of finding the beloved in the dark night of her spirit. She turns to pious persons who also have been searching for Christ and yet are not as advanced as she is. She earlier had turned to them, the daughters of Jerusalem, but now in greater humility, she charges them, that if they should find her beloved, all they should tell him is that she is love-sick for him and him alone.

St. Ambrose well describes the ardent longing of the devout soul that seeks only Christ:

The devout soul has only one true desire—her sweet Spouse Jesus. She longs for Him with all the yearnings of her heart and she goes toward Him with all her strength...so that the more ardently she longs to be united with Him, the greater are her sighs and faints. Although this fainting reduces the strength of her body, it increases and fortifies all the virtues of her spirit....The soul who denies herself in all things, so as to be perfectly united with Christ, does in fact suffer a kind of fainting.[32]

In this stage suffering and longing for greater oneness with Christ, the contemplative finds that such interior anguish at longing so passionately to be one with her beloved and yet experiencing only separation takes a heavy toll on the mental and physical well-being of the individual. Fainting is a frequent happening and a general weakness of body energy. Yet there can be no relief; she can only stay in the interior of her heart, the "cell," and, in the darkness of the consciousness and unconscious, cry out in a love-sick plaint that the beloved appear and save her from destruction.

The Chorus:

> What makes your Beloved better than other lovers,
> O loveliest of women?
> What makes your Beloved better than other lovers,
> to give us a charge like this (5:9).

1.   The daughters of Jerusalem look at the bride and ask her to tell them about her beloved. They call her loveliest of women. They, too, have been seeking him, but have not reflected a beauty to equal hers and they want her to instruct them. They can see she is different than they are and they want to have her experience of the beloved. Spiritual sufferings always draw out the interior beauty the Spirit fashions, as it divinizes the human person into the image and likeness of Christ and allows others to glimpse something of that beauty.

The daughters praise her, but now she is centered totally on her spouse. At an earlier stage of her spiritual journey she may have paused to reflect upon the compliment paid her about her spiritual beauty. But in the night of purification she is losing her self-consciousness, the awareness that she can exist as a thinking subject with anything she could claim as her own. She is entering into a oneness with no separation from her beloved. "I am Thou; Thou art I" is her experience of new oneness. She has no identity or existence by herself. She truly lives and moves and has her being in Christ (Acts 17:28).

2.   What makes your beloved better than other lovers is the same question Christ asks his followers: "But you, who do you say I am?" (Mt 16:15). How do you answer those who do not know Christ as you do? Is he a mere man, a lover among lovers? Who is he to you? What can you tell others of your intimate experience of Jesus? Truly you can only answer this through the working of the Holy Spirit as Jesus promises to send him to reveal all you need to know about him: "But the Advocate, the Holy Spirit, whom the Father will send in my name, will teach you everything and remind you of all I have said to you" (Jn 14:26).

The Bride:

> My Beloved is fresh and ruddy,
> to be known among ten thousand.
> His head is golden, purest gold,
> his locks are palm fronds
> and black as the raven.
> His eyes are doves
> at a pool of water,
> bathed in milk,
> at rest on a pool.
> His cheeks are beds of spices,
> banks sweetly scented.
> His lips are lilies,
> distilling pure myrrh.
> His hands are golden, rounded,
> set with jewels of Tarshish.
> His belly a block of ivory
> covered with sapphires.
> His legs are alabaster columns
> set in sockets of pure gold.
> His appearance is that of Lebanon,
> unrivalled as the cedars.
> His conversation is sweetness itself,

he is altogether lovable.
Such is my Beloved, such is my friend,
O daughters of Jerusalem (5:10-16).

His Is the Fullness of Life

1.   The bride begins to tell the bystanders what her beloved is like. When the groom described her beauties, they were more interior. The bride seeks to compare his beauties from his exterior features. She begins to describe him as radiant and ruddy with a healthy mien. He ranks above ten thousand, a Semitic way of expressing that he is above all other men in beauty. He possesses the fullness of life (Jn 10:10). She has chosen him above all other creatures, as his heavenly Father has also chosen him above all the children of men as his beloved Son in whom he is well pleased (Mt 3:17).

The psalmist describes the coming of the Messiah:

"Of all men you are the most handsome,
your lips are moist with grace,
for God has blessed you for ever" (Ps 45:2).

He is the

"reflection of the eternal light,
untarnished mirror of God's active power,
image of his goodness" (Wis 7:26).

St. Paul gives an outstanding description of the spouse of the Christian believer in both his divinity and his humanity:

He is the image of the unseen God
and the first-born of all creation,
for in him were created
all things in heaven and on earth:
everything visible and everything invisible...
all things were created through him and for him.
Before anything was created, he existed,
and he holds all things in unity.
Now the Church is his body,
he is its head.

As he is the Beginning,
he was first to be born from the dead,

so that he should be first in every way;
because God wanted all perfection
to be found in him
and all things to be reconciled through him and for
  him,
everything in heaven and everything on earth,
when he made peace
by his death on the cross (Col 1:15-20).

This is he who holds out to you the call to enter into mystical union with him: he who is both God from all eternity and yet the fairest of all humans. In him there is no darkness; he is light; he is the fullness of being. And yet for love of you he has entered into the darkness of this world to take upon himself your weaknesses and sinfulness. This most beautiful person of all still lives and walks into your life. By the "game" of the Resurrection, he actually lives within you. By his Spirit he wishes ardently that you experience how perfect is his love for you. He calls you to share in the nuptial union as his bride. But he also calls you to be healed of your brokenness through his personal love for you in order that you may offer yourself as a channel for his healing love to go out and touch others in your world so that they, too, may share somewhat in the oneness you possess with him. Truly with the bride you can say to Christ as the soldiers of King David said to him: "...but you, you are the equal of ten thousand of us" (2 Sm 18:3).

His Head Is Purest Gold

1.   The bride now begins to describe the physical features of her beloved, starting with his head and hair. "His head is golden, purest gold." Gold in scripture is a symbol of divinity. That Christ's head is covered with purest gold could only mean he shares in the fullness of the divinity of his Father, as St. Paul writes: "In his body lives the fullness of divinity, and in him you too find your own fulfillment in the one who is the head of every Sovereignty and Power" (Col 2:9-10). Again St. Paul writes that "Christ is the head of every man...and God is the head of Christ" (1 Cor 11:3). You as bride of Christ profess that he is more than mere man. He is truly God, light from light, as the Nicene Creed

formulates his shared divinity with the Father. But you also profess that he whose head is of purest gold, perfect divinity, without any diminishment, is also your head. He is your ultimate authority, for to obey him is to enter into a sharing in divinity. He and the Father will come and abide in you if you obey his commands (Jn 14:23).

2. The hair of the Bridegroom is described as short and curly, not like the bride who has long and plaited hair. The hair can stand for the humanity which covers the golden head of divinity in Christ. It is in his humanity that the Savior laid down his life for love of us and gained the palm of victory over our enemies and redeemed us from eternal damnation.

3. His hair, black as the raven, signifies Christ's eternal youthfulness. White hair is a sign of older adulthood and old age and a symbol of the wisdom that goes with having lived a long life. But black symbolizes the strength and attractiveness of a young man in his prime of life. And of this life we have all received from Jesus who has come so that we might have it more abundantly (Jn 10:10). He restores us to youthfulness in spirit after having been brought into the decrepitude and immobility of old age, the age of the old creation, that "has been groaning in one great act of giving birth" (Rom 8:22). This "creation still retains the hope of being freed, like us, from its slavery to decadence, to enjoy the same freedom and glory as the children of God" (Rom 8:21).

You have already shared in this new creation by being one in Christ: "And for anyone who is in Christ, there is a new creation; the old creation has gone, and now the new one is here. It is all God's work. It was God who reconciled us to himself through Christ..." (2 Cor 5:17-18). Your joy is that Christ has put you on the level of mutuality with him. You, too, have a share in his perennial youthfulness, which no sin or death can take from you as long as you abide in him.

Eyes of Doves

1. The groom has compared his bride's eyes to those of doves (1:15;4:1). The eyes of human beings, animals and birds indicate

interior qualities of the creature. As you look into the eyes of another, you can detect whether the person is loving and compassionate, or is one who hates or fears. Here the bride compares the eyes of her beloved to those of doves. Such a bird is simple, loving and pure. That is one reason why it was chosen in the Jewish law of purification as a fitting sacrifice (Lv 1:14;Lk 2:24).

Christ is full of the Holy Spirit, who is represented often in scripture as a dove. The Spirit anointed Jesus with the fullness of the Father's love, which gave him eyes so tender in their expression of love to his beloved. His eyes, the bride is saying, have looked upon her with pure, totally dedicated love.

2.   The doves are pictured as being at a pool of water. The work of the Holy Spirit is to purify the bride of Christ in a cleansing of love. Jesus must have had this thought in mind when he stood up in the outer court of the Temple in Jerusalem on the feast of the Tabernacles and cried out in a loud voice: "If any man is thirsty, let him come to me! Let the man come and drink who believes in me! As scripture says: From his breast shall flow fountains of living water" (Jn 7:38).

3.   His eyes are therefore like pools of living water that cleanse the bride of all fears, isolation and self-centeredness. They shine like dark pupils encircled by milky white as the bride seeks to describe them.

4.   His eyes described as being "at rest on a pool," are well placed in the face, like jewels well set. Such eyes the bride surely has experienced at close range as instruments of tender love for her.

Radiant Face

1.   The bride speaks of her beloved's cheeks and lips. When he spoke previously of his bride's beauty he used nine different spices to describe it (4:14). Here she merely describes his cheeks as a bed of spices. If we are convinced that our inner beauty does reflect itself exteriorly, then such beauty is mirrored also in our physical carriage, the way we walk and talk, as well as upon our face. The cheeks tell others of our physical condition and even of what may be happening on a psychic and spiritual level. With

a fever, our cheeks will be flushed. We may blush in embarrassment. In old age our cheeks may wrinkle. Pale cheeks may indicate a state of anemia. A defective liver may turn the cheeks yellow.

How the beauty of Christ must have been reflected in his humanity, especially in the features of his face! No man had ever spoken as he (Jn 7:46). "And he won the approval of all, and they were astonished by the gracious words that came from his lips" (Lk 4:22). Yet those same cheeks and that same beautiful face were beaten and spit upon for love of us:

> I offered my back to those who struck me,
> my cheeks to those who tore at my beard;
> I did not cover my face against insult and spittle
> (Is 50:5-6).

You, as Christ's bride, cannot but look upon his human face and see great beauty, because you have also contemplated that beauty disfigured to prove his love for you.

> As the crowds were appalled on seeing him
> —so disfigured did he look
> that he seemed no longer human...(Is 52:14)

Yet these cheeks are compared to most fragrant spices that attract all who smell his fragrance.

2.   His lips are lilies, distilling pure myrrh. The lilies represented here could be the red lily common in Syria or they could refer to the white lily. In the latter comparison, we see pure lips that pour out words of simplicity and the purity of love of God and neighbor. The red lily indicates the flaming love of Christ shown in his sermons and in the language used to express what flowed out of his heart in love for all of us. We have already seen the image of myrrh used often before to indicate a spice producing exquisite fragrance, but also symbolizing humility and suffering. All his spoken words, whether to the sinful woman, "Go, your sins are forgiven," or to Lazarus, "Come forth," or to the crowds, "Come to me, all you who are heavily burdened and I will refresh you," came out of his heart, the heart "nearest to the Father's

heart" (Jn 1:18). His heart was filled with love, and he was ready to sacrifice himself on the cross for that love. His lips spoke of union, but also of the suffering necessary that you and I might attain such union.

Golden Hands

1. His hands are described as made of gold, well-rounded and set with jewels of Tarshish. Gold is the symbol of divinity. The hands of Christ are the outreach of what is within, and here the image well describes his actions toward others that flow out of his divinity. He is fully man who can touch us, embrace us, be wounded in his hands by nails on the cross, give us the bread of life to eat. Yet he is fully God as well, giving us the way to the heavenly Father through the gift of his Holy Spirit. Christ's hands are rounded, like a lotus blossom that open up in a circular movement of self-giving to all who come to him.

These hands were set with rare jewels from Tarshish. One such jewel, some commentators believe, was the beryl stone which was set in gold on the high priest's breastplate when he acted as mediator on behalf of the people of Israel (Ex 28:20). As Moses stretched out his arms and hands upward to God on behalf of his people in battle against the Amalekites and his soldiers were victorious as long as he was in intercessory prayer (Ex 17:11), so Christ is our high priest whose hands are held up to the Father in prayer for us. Those hands are set with the rare jewels of his wounds by which we are to be healed (Is 53:5). You have as your perfect mediator, your groom, Jesus Christ: "For there is only one God, and there is only one mediator between God and mankind, himself a man, Christ Jesus, who sacrificed himself as a ransom for them all" (1 Tm 2:5-6). He is our advocate (1 Jn 2:1) and the heavenly Father always grants his petitions on our behalf. How consoling it is to know that day and night Jesus, our beloved, is interceding before the Father's throne for us. The victory is assured! Nothing can harm us, for he who is within us is more powerful than any force outside of us (1 Jn 4:4). "But this one, because he remains for ever, can never lose his priesthood. It follows, then, that his power to save is utterly certain, since he is living for ever to intercede for all who come to God through him" (Heb 7:24-25).

His Body—A Temple

1.   Once Jesus spoke to the Pharisees: " 'Destroy this sanctuary, and in three days I will raise it up.'...But he was speaking of the sanctuary that was his body" (Jn 2:19-22). No doubt the original writer(s) of the *Song*, especially in this description of the bridegroom, had wanted to describe Yahweh as the groom and Israel as his bride. Yahweh was among his people, loving and protecting them by his presence especially in his Temple in Jerusalem. When God's Word became incarnate, when he pitched his tent (sanctuary) among them (Jn 1:14), Jesus Christ replaced the Temple.

Keeping this primary comparison in mind we can apply the various images of the Temple to the human body of Christ. "His belly a block of ivory covered with sapphires." Jesus' belly refers to the source of his life, the "bowels" (Jn 7:38) of his being out of which come love and compassion. Bright ivory, a symbol of purity and innocence, suggests that his humanity had to undergo much suffering to be polished so as to glisten with a spotlessly clean and pure love for us all.

2.   "...covered with sapphires" suggests to us the blue color of heaven, reflecting Christ's heavenly and perfect virtues. For when he suffered out of love for us in his white, stark body hanging on the cross, he was still God suffering. God was dying for us! This is the good news that thrills the bride of Christ.

Legs Like Alabaster Columns

1.   "His legs are alabaster columns set in sockets of pure gold." Christ was Oriental in his humanity and, therefore, alabaster rather than white marble is a more fitting color for the polished stone chosen to depict his foundation. But we build our faith, not merely on his beautiful humanity, but on the fact that he, Jesus Christ, is both man and God. His humanity, like legs strong as alabaster columns, is set into his divinity as in sockets of pure gold. Christ saves us in his humanity, but because he is truly "God from God, of one substance with the Father." St. Paul clearly gives

our profession of faith when he wrote: "In his body lives the fullness of divinity, and in him you too find your own fulfillment, in the one who is the head of every Sovereignty and Power" (Col 2:9-10).

For that reason, although Christ died, he did not see corruption (Acts 2:31), but both his humanity and divinity were raised to a new glory. As his bride, you, too, profess that you love a total man, but he is also God!

2. The bride compares her beloved to the high cedars on the heights of Mount Lebanon. So does Christ stand supreme above all human persons. He is unrivaled. No one can hold for us, his brides, any comparable competition for the exclusive attachment we give to Christ.

He Is Totally Lovable

1. The beloved's mouth is said to be sweetness itself to the bride. This is a way of describing Christ's speech. What comes out of his mouth are sweet words of love, even if they are meant to reprove us and call us away from selfishness. He is the Word of God and every word that Christ utters comes from the mind of the Father.

Such words should be most sweet to you, his bride, for they pour out of God's very heart. The words of Christ are symbols that enflesh in sound what lies deeply within the depths of God's eternal love for you.

2. No wonder you and I, overwhelmed by Christ's beauty in the communication of his love for us, can become delirious about his beauty as we explain: "He is altogether lovable." We can never love him enough, for at every moment he utters words most sweet by which we become more and more ravished by his love. We understand with shuddering awe, humility and excitement that this all-perfect God-man belongs to each of us, totally and completely, as our unique beloved!

My Beloved, My Friend

1. The bride seems to come to an end of all she wishes to tell the daughters of Jerusalem. There is so much more to say, but she turns to silence as she concludes: "Such is my Beloved, such is my friend, O daughters of Jerusalem." What more can the bride say than what she has already said about the beauties of her beloved? She again calls him her beloved and her friend. She seems to invite the daughters so that they, too, can possess him as their beloved and friend. Love begets love. But love of Christ selfishly possessed exclusively for oneself and not shared so others can receive the same happiness is no true love at all. We want the whole world to know Christ as we do. We can only describe his beauties to others in proportion as we have truly experienced him as our beautiful beloved and friend. But once you have entered into an intimate union with him as his bride, it becomes easy to present his beauty to others so they will eagerly want to discover what has been your experience.

Chapter Six

The Chorus:

> Where did your Beloved go,
> O loveliest of women?
> Which way did your Beloved turn
> so that we can help you to look for him?

The Bride:

> My Beloved went down to his garden,
> to the beds of spices,
> to pasture his flock in the gardens
> and gather lilies.
> I am my Beloved's, and my Beloved is mine.
> He pastures his flock among the lilies (6:1-3).

1.   The Chorus, made up of daughters of Jerusalem, symbolizes other Christians, eager to follow Christ, yet not far advanced in mystical intimacy with the groom. In the exchange, we see the power of the Holy Spirit to touch other persons through a Christian who speaks to them out of intimate experience with Christ. We have seen these "daughters of Jerusalem" earlier in the *Song* berating the bride as though she were insane. Now they have

been touched by her sincerity, example and fervor in speaking about the beauties of Christ whom she knows so intimately, and they eagerly wish to find him, too.

The power of Christianity converts seekers, not by rational arguments, but by such a Christian as the bride, inebriated with the new life that Christ has brought her through his Spirit. There is a fire communicated from such a person to those who are disposed but have not yet known Christ intimately in the depths of their hearts. St. Augustine knew that all human beings will always be restless, seeking Christ who alone can satisfy the human heart.

Loveliest of Women

2.   They now call the bride the "loveliest of women." True seekers of Christ will be able by the power of his Spirit to recognize the beauty of Christ in another who is more united to him than they are. And they have a "holy envy" to become lovely and beautiful as the contemplative bride. Complimenting a holy person who radiates Christ, such a one says in substance: "How can I be like you? I want what you have. Lead me to the source of your beauty."

3.   They ask the bride where her beloved has gone so they can help find him. They imply that he has temporarily left her, but that she knows where he has gone. They will travel together to find him, but it will be she, the bride, who has more knowledge than they, the less advanced, who will lead them to him. The spiritual direction of leading others to Christ comes best from those who are well experienced in his ways and habitually moving under the inspiration of his Holy Spirit.

The Inner Garden

1.   The bride witnesses to those with her that her beloved is not outside, but that he lives within the garden of her heart. She herself, after earlier attempts to find him outside in the "city," has now been led by him through various inner and exterior purifications to realize that he lives all the time at the core and center of her being. Being now so surrendered to his wishes, she is given an even greater awareness that he is within her.

115

2. She professes that deep within her the beloved is found at the garden bed of spices, working to produce in her the fragrance of his virtues. There he pastures his sheep by feeding each one individually with the nourishing gift of himself as food and drink.

3. And there he gathers lilies. Christ loves the pure of heart. They truly see him within their hearts. They also are able to some degree to see him in others and in the entire world, shining "diaphanously," in Teilhard de Chardin's phrase, for all who have the eyes to see him.

The Beloved Is Mine

1. We see the great change that has come to the bride in her awareness of how totally she now belongs to her beloved and he to her. Earlier, even while she was still holding on to him out of a desire for his sweetnesses and consolations, she claimed, "My Beloved is mine and I am his" (2:16). Now she has been led away from herself as the focus to surrender totally to him. She is ready in her purity to follow him in any way he wishes to guide her. Her happiness is to surrender to him and obey his leadings.

When such a union with Christ is reached, then you can cry out with St. Paul:

> For I am certain of this: neither death nor life, no angel, no prince, nothing that exists, nothing still to come, not any power, or height or depth, nor any created thing, can ever come between us and the love of God made visible in Christ Jesus our Lord (Rom 8:38-39).

In such a new consciousness, Christ's mystical bride lives in an inner world of love, peace, joy and gentleness, all fruits of the Holy Spirit. She radiates to all whom she meets and in all circumstances an inner exultation of infectious joy. For she has truly passed beyond the world she has created to enter into God's reality and to see everything bathed in the brilliant light of Christ. She has completely died to herself and knows with absolute certitude from the Spirit that she belongs to Christ. Now she knows she can never lose him, because she has lost her greatest enemy to union with him, her false ego. She can never lose this new life, for she has died to all elements that might drive away him who is "the Way, the Truth and the Life" (Jn 14:6).

St. Bernard in his commentary on the *Song* writes of such advanced comtemplatives:

> This is what perfect souls say: Who these are is known to God; but you must listen so that you can reach such happiness...Give me a soul who loves only God and those things related to Him that should be loved, who can not only say that her life is in Christ, but who for some time has had Christ dwelling within her, who in her works and holy repose longs only to have the Lord always before her eyes to conform to His most holy will in all things; give me such a soul as this, and I assure you that she will be worthy of the Spouse's care and of His Divine Majesty's favors and attentions.[33]

Fifth Poem

The Bridegroom:

You are beautiful as Tirzah, my love,
fair as Jerusalem.
Turn your eyes away,
for they hold me captive.
Your hair is like a flock of goats
frisking down the slopes of Gilead.
Your teeth are like a flock of sheep
as they come up from the washing.
Each one has its twin,
not one unpaired with another.
Your cheeks, behind your veil,
are halves of pomegranate.

There are sixty queens
and eighty concubines
(and countless maidens).
But my dove is unique,
mine, unique and perfect.
She is the darling of her mother,
the favorite of the one who bore her.
The maidens saw her, and proclaimed her blessed,
queens and concubines sang her praises:
"Who is this arising like the dawn,
fair as the moon,
resplendent as the sun,
terrible as an army with banners?"

I went down to the nut orchard
to see what was sprouting in the valley,
to see if the vines were budding
and the pomegranate trees in flower.

> Before I knew...my desire had hurled me
> on the chariots of my people, as their prince (6:4-12).

The Fair Bride

1.   Pleased with the bride's enthusiastic praise of him to the daughters of Jerusalem, the bridegroom again praises his beloved. He already spoke of her beauty and comeliness. Now he describes her beauty after the many purifications that have led her not only to a deeper union with him, but also to a new harmony and integration within herself.

He compares her beauty to the city of Tirzah.[34] This city symbolizes the Northern Kingdom which Jeroboam established as his capital after the schism. St. Athanasius sees Tirzah as referring to the Gentiles, and Jerusalem referring to the Jews, while the bride is the church of Christ, united in one body. We might see the reference to the bride's beauty compared to the two ancient cities of Tirzah and Jerusalem as the mystical bride of Christ brought by Christ's great love for her into a union of the divine and the human.

The Christian bride has her natural beauty, symbolized by the city of Tirzah, transformed through Christ's love for her. She shares in his divinity, symbolized by Jerusalem, God's presence as the Heavenly City on this earth. She is "as beautiful as a bride all dressed for her husband" (Rv 21:2).

Christ's love transforms the Christian through sufferings and trials into a bride most beautiful and powerful, as symbolized by these two cities. Love begets love and the Lover transforms the beloved to enable her to share his qualities. Christ not only rejoices to see his image reflected in the Christian contemplative, but he eagerly wishes to receive the bride's beauty as a new love, a personal gift of herself to him.

Captivating Eyes

1.   The beloved is so captivated by the bride's newly developed beauty, especially as he gazes into her eyes, that he says: "Turn your eyes away, for they hold me captive." God often employs a stratagem of asking a holy person to turn away from exercising a power of intercession that he or she only persists even more

to entreat him. Yahweh told Moses to stop asking him to forgive his sinful people: "Leave me, now!" (Ex 32:10). God in the form of an angel wrestled with Jacob all through the night and at dawn begged him to let him go: "Let me go for day is breaking" (Gn 32:26). Jesus seemingly turned away from the powerful pleas of the Syro-Phoenician woman so she would persist in her pleading (Mk 7:26-29). How powerful is the plea of Christ's bride to touch his heart and obtain from him whatever she asks (Jn 15:7).

2. But this passage can have a deeper meaning for the mystical bride of Christ. If his spirit has transformed her into a beauty that completely ravishes Christ, we might see this, not as a wish or command, but as an expression of how passionate is Christ's love for his bride. He has espoused himself to her. She has surrendered herself completely to him. The two see themselves as one. Such a love experienced by Christ in his human-divine personhood calls him into new levels of uniqueness in his love for his bride. Such ecstatic discovery leads Christ to describe how much her love means to him. He begs her to stop gazing on him with such a look of surrendering love, but he knows she never will turn away. She belongs to him and he to her. What blessed pain to possess so much new being in union with another that the beloved can only ask, as St. Francis of Assisi cried out in ecstatic oneness with Christ: "It is too much!" Yet the true lover and beloved know it can never be too much.

Increased Perfection

1. We may find it strange that the author of the *Song* now repeats what was said by the groom about the bride's physical beauty of hair, teeth and cheeks in 4:1-4. One reason may be that love always begets a new release of beauty. What the bridegroom earlier saw of beauty in his bride he now sees as more fully visible and more easily witnessed to by his beloved.

Her hair, a symbol of her thoughts, is again described as a flock of frisky goats down the slopes of Gilead. Through deeper union with Christ, the Christian bride has put aside her vain and ego-centered thoughts as so much disheveled hair. Now she delights in her beloved with only one ordered thought—how to please him in total surrender.

2.   Her teeth are like a flock of sheep as they come up from the washing. Each tooth is evenly "twined" with another. By her clean and orderly teeth she is able to eat and chew well the word of God. She chews the bread of life and the substantial meat of Christ's word so as to be nourished to live as his bride and nourish others as she shares God's word with them.

3.   Her cheeks, behind her veil, are like two halves of pomegranate. How much more now the bride in her hidden, veiled self builds her true beauty on the passion and death of Christ. Yet her cheeks, her exterior behavior toward others, cannot but reflect her inner beauty. She inwardly has progressively died to self in holy surrender to the purifications Christ arranged in her life. Now one with him in nuptial union, her joy in suffering all things with him and out of love for him and her reflected Christ-beauty are seen by others.

Unique and Perfect Dove

1.   The groom continues to praise the beauty of his bride. He compares her to others, to those who have a relationship to the king. The reference to King Solomon (1 Kgs 11:3) highlights numerous persons who serve the king in varying degrees of intimacy. A Christian interpretation sees the 60 queens, 80 concubines and countless maidens as referring to various categories of dedicated Christians who seek the mystical union that Christ holds out to all his followers.

If God truly "wants everyone to be saved and reach full knowledge of the truth" (1 Tm 2:5) and if Jesus has died for all persons that we might all have eternal life (Jn 3:16), then God wants all his children to experience a mystical oneness with Christ. Yet such a life in Christ admits of beginners, intermediates and the more advanced. Christians who have already entered into the contemplative life and know a oneness with Christ dwelling within them, divide still more into three groups. There are those who are brought into an equality by God's transforming grace—the "queens" or the true wives of the king who share most intimately with Christ and are recognized by others publicly as his intimates. They beget his true children.

The concubines are those who by grace share also in the intimacy of the queens; they bring him equal satisfaction and joy but do not have the public status and honors of being his queens. These number more that the queens, indicating the numerous hidden souls who please Christ and live in the greatest intimacy with him.

The "countless maidens" could refer to the many contemplative persons who have entered into Christ's palace and have been led into the first rooms, but not yet the bedroom of greatest intimacy as bride of the groom. These are like the good and foolish virgins who have been called to wait for the coming of the bridegroom. Some of these will continue to grow by their vigilance and burning desire to surrender themselves totally to whatever Christ asks of them, and they will be led ever more progressively into the inner chambers of intimacy with him. Others will yield to diversions in their following of Christ and will hear the words of the Savior: "I tell you solemnly, I do not know you" (Mt 25:13).

My Dove Is Perfect

1.   The groom says something new for the first time. His bride was earlier compared to a dove, pure and single-eyed in her complete dedication to him. But now he says she is unique and perfect. God spoke to Abraham in similar terms of endearment: "Take your son, your only (unique) child Isaac, whom you love..." (Gn 22:2). Christ, as the groom, declares that his bride is unique. As his body, the church, his bride is one, an integrated entity that has been made perfect by the grace of his Holy Spirit. She is spotless, without stain or blemish:

> He made her clean by washing her in water with a form of words, so that when he took her to himself she would be glorious, with no speck or wrinkle or anything like that, but holy and faultless (Eph 5:26-27).

2.   Yet the unique bride is also every human person who has answered his call to follow him perfectly by obeying all his wishes: "We are its living parts" (Eph 5:31). You can become the one, perfect bride of Christ, not in a quantitative sense that you alone

are his bride, but in a qualitative sense as having reached a oneness with Christ, an integration of yourself in Christ, a fulfillment of God's image and likeness as he first created you to be, perfect in Christ. Your perfection is Christ's perfection in you, his grace made full in you as you enter into the mystical oneness with him. It will allow you to see his perfect love, his Spirit, as your very own love returned as perfect, only because it is all his Spirit's work. You become perfect interiorly by your free choice to die to all your self-seeking, as you ardently seek only to surrender to his wishes.

3.   Christ declares that you, his bride, are "the darling" of your mother, "the favorite" of the one who bore you (6:8). All Christians who allow Christ's Spirit freely to operate in them are the favorites of the mother, the church, who begot them into God's life. The church is our mother because Christ has given her through his Spirit all power in his commission to preach his word, to administer his sacraments and to guide us infallibly into the truth. We become the favorite of such a mother by becoming in miniature form what she stands for: the bride of Christ, through total surrender to God's word. "I am the handmaid of the Lord. let what you have said be done to me" (Lk 1:38).

She Is Blessed

1.   It is still the groom who declares that the maidens who saw her "proclaimed her blessed; queens and concubines sang her praises" (6:9). The difference between the maidens and the queens and concubines refers to those who have not yet advanced far in the spiritual life as compared to those who have already entered into conjugal intimacy with the king. Both groups are struck by the bride's blessedness and they sing her praises.

How beautifully Christ, the groom, declares what Mary declared with great humility about herself: "Yes, from this day forward all generations will call me blessed, for the Almighty has done great things for me. Holy is his name" (Lk 1:48-49). A sign of true followers of Christ, whether beginners or the more advanced, is the joy that comes to them at seeing the workings of Christ's Spirit in a chosen soul completely surrendered to him.

2. In the Book of Revelation we hear the praises of the bystanders around Christ and his bride beautifully expressing what already exists in the bride and what will yet in the life to come:

> And I seemed to hear the voices of a huge crowd, like the sound of the ocean or the great roar of thunder, answering "Alleluia! The reign of the Lord our God Almighty has begun; let us be glad and joyful and give praise to God, because this is the time for the marriage of the Lamb. His Bride is ready, and she has been able to dress herself in dazzling white linen, because her linen is made of the good deeds of the saints"(Rv 9:6-9).

Arising Like the Dawn

1. The maidens, queens and concubines praise the beauty of the bride of Christ by posing four comparisons as a challenge to others who have not advanced as far as she has in union with Christ. Who is she who rises like the dawn? We have all stood transfixed by the beauty of the early morning sunrise. The sun gradually appears on the horizon as a faint glimmer of light. The light deepens to pink, deep red and then bursts upon the world as a ball of flame.

The bride's beauty is compared to the gradual rising of the dawn. There is no longer any darkness in her. She has heard St. Paul's advice: "Let us arm ourselves and appear in the light" (Rom 13:13). The night of living in the darkness of her own desires is over and Christ is now her light (Jn 9:5). He is "the Sun of Righteousness" (Mal 3:20). And she shares in his light, but only as the early morning dawn shares in the sun's light until the morn reaches high noon:

> The path of the virtuous is like the light of dawn,
> its brightness growing to the fullness of day" (Pr 4:18).

Fair as the Moon

1. The bride is complimented by the other women as being "fair as the moon" (6:10). Christ's bride is beautiful because she reflects the beauty of Christ. As the moon receives all its gentle, soft light

from the sun, so the bride has all her beauty from the light of Christ. All who truly are united to Christ reflect his light of beauty to others. "In the same way your light must shine in the sight of men, so that, seeing your good works, they may give the praise to your Father in heaven" (Mt 5:16).

This is the witness to the world that lies in darkness to Christ's lightsome presence which contemplative Christians give to others. Seeing their soft light, they can be led to the full light of Christ:

> ...enduring for ever like the moon,
> that faithful witness in the sky (Ps 89:37).

Resplendent as the Sun

1. By being compared to the moon, the bride reflects the full gratuitous gifts of God operating in her. Now she is described as "resplendent as the sun" to indicate that it is still *her* beauty that she offers to others to attract them to Christ. It is her deep union with Christ that allows others to see her beauty and also to see implicitly the source of that light and beauty, Christ. All men and women, created by God in Christ's image, yearn to come out of darkness into his light. Yet all of us need persons who, in their beautiful love for God and for others, bring us to long for perfect beauty in Christ.

An Army with Banners

1. The bride is praised for being "terrible as an army with banners" (6:10). She in her weakness and humility knows that all her strength is in Christ who makes her, even now, share in his victory over sin and death "You have in you one who is greater than anyone in this world" (1 Jn 4:4).

She is awesome to others who see her strength from within due to the indwelling presence of the Lord Jesus who strengthens her. She is like an army with banners unfurled, already a sign of victory over devils, the world and the flesh, over all sin and self-love.

Down to the Nut Orchard

1. Verses 11 and 12 of chapter 6 present us with a very confusing text both as to who speaks these lines and to their significance.

Let us follow the majority of modern commentators who attribute them to the bridegroom. The images found in these verses are loaded with symbols indicating sexual union and fertility.[35] Christ here, after having praised the beauty of his bride and told of his passionate desires for her, says that he went down to the nut orchard "to see what was sprouting in the valley, to see if the vines were budding and the pomegranate trees in flower" (6:11).

The bride has entered into the valley of darkness and death. Through the trials and purifications endured by her to prepare her for her mystical marriage with her beloved, she is waiting, with the readiness of vines in bud and pomegranate trees in blossom, for full union with Christ.

2.   The images of nuts to be cracked open to yield to fruit, pruned vines and grapes to be crushed into wine, and pomegranates with red fruit like blood poured out speak of how Christ went into the Garden of Gethsemani to prepare for his loving surrendering on our behalf through sufferings. They speak also of the need for his bride to be fertile and fruitful in union with Christ by sharing in his sufferings, "still to be undergone by Christ for the sake of his body, the Church" (Col 1:24).

A Burning Desire

1.   The groom confesses to a sudden burst of love for his bride. It was beyond his controlled rationality, as he says in this verse, "Before I knew..." (6:12), that Christ in his burning love for his people was "hurled" into his passion, death and resurrection. We can see something of this "beyond knowledge" in the great love in the heart of Christ before he went to his death for his bride:

> Jesus knew that the hour had come for him to pass from this world to the Father. He had always loved those who were his in the world, but now he showed how perfect his love was (Jn 13:1).

Periodically during his public life this flaming love in his heart to accomplish what his Father had sent him to do would flare out in words of ardent longing: "I have come to bring fire to the earth and how I wish it were blazing already! There is a baptism I must still receive, and how great is my distress till it is over!" (Lk

12:49-50). His baptism would be of water and blood poured out from his loving heart, the heart of the suffering God, imaged in Jesus, for his bride.

The horrendous folly of the sufferings of Christ is sheer nonsense except in terms of the logic of divine love! For the contemplative, Christ, poor in spirit, in his awful *kenosis* or self-emptying even to the last drop of blood and water, has fullest meaning only in being an exact *image* of the heart of God the Father in his infinite, tender, self-sacrificing love for each individual.

We as human beings would always have entertained some doubt as to the infinite love of the Father for us unless he who so loved us as to give us his only-begotten Son (Jn 3:16) was being imaged perfectly in Jesus poured out unto the last drop of water and blood! In Jesus, "finished" on the cross, not only do we reach the end of his earthly life, but we reach the *end* of God's giving of himself to us. For not even God can speak another word beyond his Word spoken in utter emptying unto death in Jesus. Beyond creative suffering unto death there is no other language in which both human and divine love can be adequately expressed. He loves us with the love of the Father for us:

> "As the Father has loved me,
> so I have loved you" (Jn 15:9).

2.   The bride's beloved says: "My desire had hurled me on the chariots of my people, as their prince." We are presented with a double imagery. First, we can see how the phrase, "the chariots of my people," can refer to Christ's chosen followers as they move forward in their attack-chariots to do battle against the forces of evil led by Satan and his cohorts. Yet Christ now is risen. He has been raised in glory by the Father and to him has been given dominion over sun and death and all other adverse powers:

> He has put all things under his feet, and made him,
> as the ruler of everything, the head of the Church,
> which is his body, the fullness of him who fills the
> whole creation (Eph 1:22-23).

But Christ also, as declared in this text, is called *prince* of his people. This has eschatological overtones denoting the cosmic Christ who will lead them back from the long battles on earth. His army of chosen warriors will be presented to his heavenly Father. Through them Christ will come again leading the whole cosmos as completed by entering into his body, the church.

Christ is already prince of the world. But his decisive victory over the cosmic powers of evil requires extension in space and time in order to reach all persons and all creatures in all places. "Yet, in keeping with his promise we look for new heavens and a new earth, in which holiness dwells" (2 Pt 3:13).

Chapter Seven

The Chorus:

> Return, return, O maid of Shulam,
> return, return, that we may gaze on you!

The Bridegroom:

> Why do you gaze on the maid of Shulam
> dancing as though between two rows of dancers?
>
> How beautiful are your feet in their sandals,
> O prince's daughter!
> The curve of your thighs is like the curve of a necklace,
> work of a master hand.
> Your navel is a bowl well rounded
> with no lack of wine,
> your belly a heap of wheat
> surrounded with lilies.
> Your two breasts are two fawns,
> twins of a gazelle.
> Your neck is an ivory tower.
> Your eyes, the pools of Heshbon,
> by the gate of Bath-rabbim.
> Your nose, the Tower of Lebanon,
> sentinel facing Damascus.

> Your head is held high like Carmel,
> and its plaits are as dark as purple;
> a king is held captive in your tresses.
> How beautiful you are, how charming,
> my love, my delight!
> In stature like the palm tree,
> its fruit-clusters your breasts.
> "I will climb the palm tree," I resolved,
> "I will seize its clusters of dates."
> May your breasts be clusters of grapes,
> your breath sweet-scented as apples,
> your speaking, superlative wine (7:1-10).

Come Back, Shulamite

1.   The maidens of Jerusalem cry out to the bride who suddenly disappears from their view, perhaps because she is called inside to share intimately the love of her beloved. She is called the "maid of Shulam" or of Solomon (7:1). Christ, her spouse, is the new Solomon. His bride, the maidens acknowledge, shares in his chief characteristic as one who is *peaceful*. She receives his power to bring peace to others, the fruit of the Spirit's love in her heart (Gal 5:22).

They wish to look upon her in the radiant beauty she reflects from her king and spouse. They wish to study how she has entered into a oneness with her spouse so that they also may share in her reflected beauty.

A Dancing Bride

1.   The bridegroom asks the maidens why they gaze on his bride of peace: "Why do you gaze on the maid of Shulam dancing as though between two rows of dancers?" (7:1). This verse alludes to the unification of two camps or groups that had earlier been divided. In Genesis 32:2-22 Jacob or Israel returned after seven years serving Laban and divided his entourage into two camps. The text that is more completely alluded to here is from Jeremiah 31:4,12 which dramatically describes the reunion after the Babylonian exile of the two kingdoms of Israel and Judah into a single kingdom and a new covenant:

I build you once more; you shall be rebuilt,
virgin of Israel.
Adorned once more, and with your tambourines,
you will go out dancing gaily....
The virgin will then take pleasure in the dance,
young men and old will be happy;
I will change their mourning into gladness,
comfort them, give them joy after their troubles...
(Jer 31:4,13).

Christ sees his bride dancing at her wedding banquet. He has taken her who was separated before by her immaturity and self-centeredness and made her one with him, her head. As the individual Christian becomes one with Christ, so the total bride, his church, becomes the unifying power of the world of Jews and Gentiles, of males and females, of slaves and free, because "all of you are one in Christ Jesus" (Gal 3:28).

2.   Pure and virginal, living ecstatically for her beloved, the bride dances the victory dance before the two companies of other Christian warriors. She bears the aspect of strength and terror of the entire army, for she stands as an archetype of the meek and humble handmaid of the Lord through whom God "has shown the power of his arm, he has routed the proud of heart" (Lk 1:51).

Prince's Daughter

1.   The groom begins now to praise his bride as he did earlier. But then he began with her head and moved down to her feet. Now he begins by describing her feet: "How beautiful are your feet in their sandals, O prince's daughter" (7:2). The feet of his bride are beautiful because they are covered by sandals; she is ready to go everywhere to announce the good news of her beloved's love for all mankind. Faith comes from what is preached, as St. Paul writes (Rom 10:17), and what is preached comes from the word of Christ. Yet Christ sends forth his disciples to preach his good news so that others may hear and believe. St. Paul writes: "The footsteps of those who bring good news is a welcome sound" (Rom 10:15).

The bride's feet are described as in the words of the prophet Isaiah:

> How beautiful on the mountains,
> are the feet of one who brings good news,
> who heralds peace, brings happiness,
> proclaims salvation,
> and tells Zion,
> "your God is king!" (Is 52:7).

She is prepared with sandals on her feet to go wherever she can to share her love, peace and joy with others.

2.   She is called "the prince's daughter" to indicate that through Christ she has received a share in his divine inheritance: "And if we are children we are heirs as well: heirs of God and coheirs with Christ, sharing his sufferings so as to share his glory" (Rom 8:17). What an amazing miracle of God's grace, that we Christians are called to be Christ's bride insofar as through Christ's Spirit we have become truly children of God. Such a transformation, whereby we actually have become God's children by grace as Jesus is the Son of God by nature, sends us forth to share this divine inheritance with others.

To Run in the Ways of the Lord

1.   The legs or their running parts, the thighs, are described as well-rounded like the pieces of a jeweled necklace: "The curve of your thighs is like the curve of a necklace, work of a master hand" (7:2). Strong joints that fit the legs to the body and allow the athlete to run with speed and coordination here aptly describe the bride's integration in perfect obedience to move under Christ's commands.

St. Paul beautifully describes the church as a body, well-fitted and joined together, "every joint adding its own strength, for each separate part to work according to its function" (Eph 4:16).

2.   Each part of the bride fits together as the jewels of a necklace are joined together by a skilled artisan to produce a work of beauty and harmony. God creates us with all our faculties, powers and abilities to be fitted through obedience to his holy will into a well-rounded, integrated and loving submission to his will: "We

are God's work of art, created in Christ Jesus to live the good life as from the beginning he had meant us to live it" (Eph 2:10).

The Center of the World

1.   Commentators have offered a variety of interpretations of 7:3: "Your navel is a bowl well rounded with no lack of wine." The literal meaning intended by the author of the *Song* must lie in some reference to Israel as Yahweh's bride. Here, as A. Robert points out,[36] the bride's navel represents the city of Jerusalem built on a spur attached to Gareb on the northeast, but bordered on the east, south and west by deep wadis (the Kedron, Hinnom and ir-Rababy) which fashion an arc of a circle. Such an arc suggests also a crater or a "well-rounded" drinking bowl.

Tradition, both Jewish and Christian, considered Jerusalem as the center of the world. For Christians it becomes the center of the new creation, for it is in Jerusalem that Christ dies on the cross, rises and sends the Holy Spirit upon his followers to begin the new life in Christ.

The bride is described as beautiful in her navel, where spiritually she is attached to Christ, her life line, to be nourished by his new wine, his sacred blood in the Eucharist.

The Bread of Life

1.   The bridegroom praises the belly of the bride by comparing it to "a heap of wheat surrounded with lilies." The mystical bride of Christ is beautiful because spiritually she is nourished by Christ's indwelling presence who comes to her in the fullest symbol of bread and wine, body and blood, total God and total man.

2.   That "place" of harvest of mystical union between the bride and Christ is described as surrounded with lilies. The bride enters into union with Christ only in the purity of heart where she lives totally and completely for Christ. She is intoxicated by his love and sees all reality in the light of his loving presence: "Happy the pure in heart: they shall see God" (Mt 5:8).

Twin Mountains

1.   Looking at Jerusalem, the author of the *Song* sees the twin mountains of Ebal and Gerizin. He uses the image as a sign of

the prosperity and fertility of the union of the southern and northern kingdoms into one kingdom after the exile. Christian commentators saw the breasts of the bride, the church and/or the individual Christian in conscious oneness with Christ, as symbolic of love of God and love of neighbor. These two breasts of the bride "are two fawns, twins of a gazelle" (7:4).

These two loves of the bride are like little fawns which are fed by the love of Christ. As they develop, this dual love of God and neighbor reflects the speed of a gazelle. The bride is swift to obey her beloved, Christ. She turns away with greatest alertness from any impending evil or danger that might take her away from nourishing others in the love of God and zeal for neighbor.

Like an Ivory Tower

1. The neck of the bride is compared to an ivory tower: "Your neck is an ivory tower" (7:5). Earlier the groom compared the bride's neck to the tower of David (4:4), which highlighted a storehouse of weapons. Here her neck is described as strength and power, but of a refined and well-polished nature as signified by the image of ivory.

The bride has undergone long sufferings and purifications that gives her a newly acquired power of refined beauty, of inner strength because she knows now that Christ is her whole strength. In complete submission to Christ, her beloved, she becomes both pure and simple, courageous to do all things in his power. Her neck is what beautifully attaches her completely to Christ, her head.

The Eyes of the Soul

1. "Your eyes, the pools of Heshbon, by the gate of Bathrabbim" (7:5). Earlier the bride's eyes were compared to those of doves, in her simple and loving look for Christ alone. Now her eyes are compared to the beautiful, clear pools of Heshbon, an ancient Amorite royal city between Amman and Madaba, noted for its pools and reservoirs of fresh, clear water.

The bride in her pure devotion to Christ, reflects in her eyes, as in a mirror, his image which shines upon her constantly. She reflects Christ's image as the Father's love in her eyes and in all her encounters with others.

An Attentive Sentinel

1. In a rather strange comparison the bride's nose is compared to "the Tower of Lebanon, sentinel facing Damascus" (7:6). Commentators generally believe this is a comparison to Mount Hermon that faced Damascus. It could also refer to a tower called Lebanon built on Mount Hermon. At any rate, her nose is described as beautiful in its straight line from the brow downward, without any bluntness or flatness. On a deeper level, the beauty of her nose is described in terms of a sentinel facing inimical force, typified by the word, Damascus. The bride is ready to protect her beloved from any attack from his enemies.

Love always goes beyond any rational limits. It knows excesses, at least what may appear as such to the non-lover. The Christian who has entered into the ecstatic oneness with Christ loses all sense of an independent ego and lives solely for him. She is ready, with great joy, even to lay down her life to protect her spouse:

> A man can have no greater love
> than to lay down his life for his friends (Jn 15:13).

Luxuriant Hair

1. The bride's head with its luxuriant tresses is compared to Mount Carmel, which is a high and verdant mountain, rich in fruit orchards and pastures. But Mount Carmel conjured up in the mind of the Jewish reader two historical references that give us a deep meaning for the Christian bride of Christ.

It was a territory which Joshua conquered from a pagan ruler (Jos 12:22). Jesus is the conqueror of his bride, who was held captive by the enemy of darkness. But also God's chosen people fell away from Yahweh. God sent the prophet Elijah to bring his bride back and he had all the false prophets of Baal put to death (1 Kgs 18:19,40).

Another comparison that Carmel suggests could refer to Abigail, King David's favorite wife. She came from Mount Carmel

(1 Sm 27:3). She had first been the servant of Nabal, in bondage and afraid of him. After Nabal married her and died, David set her free and married her. Abigail, from a slave, became the king's ruling wife.

The good news that Jesus announces and makes possible is that he has come to set all of us free. But more so, he releases his Spirit who "divinizes" us to become truly God's very own children (1 Jn 3:1). We are made participators in God's very own nature (2 Pt 1:4). Now you and I can actually be on an equal footing with Christ. He truly can desire us, loving us with passion and longing because he finds us exceedingly beautiful. All this is a mystery of grace which we can only believe in great humility and in complete surrender to him.

2. "...and its plaits are as dark as purple" (7:6). Not only is the bride's head, her superior faculties of knowing and loving her spouse, described as rich and luxuriant, but its plaits are dark as purple. Purple in scripture is the color of royalty and divinity. The bride has truly been wedded by Christ and, therefore, reigns royally with him.

You are no longer a slave to your own false self, but Christ frees you and weds you as his co-equal. But such a sharing in his divinity and royal sonship before his heavenly Father, "co-heirs with Christ" (Rom 8:17), can take place only if you are ready to share "his sufferings so as to share his glory" (Rom 8:17). By his blood you are to put on the purple sign of royalty and divinity.

A Captive King

1. When Christ sees his Christian bride ready to surrender to his will in all things, to accept joyfully all crosses, trials and persecutions for his sake, he the king is overcome by her beauty: "A king is held captive in your tresses" (7:6). We will never understand, not only how great is Jesus' love for each of us individually, but also how much joy we give to his heart and through him to the heart of our Father. That we are capable of "captivating" the heart of our beloved and king is a mystery that overwhelms us. We would disbelieve that Jesus passionately desires us if he did not die for love of us, if he does not truly give himself totally to us in the Eucharist.

What love and humility that Jesus Christ, God-man, should actually be overcome by our beauty, the masterpiece created by his Spirit of love!

How Beautiful You Are

1.   Here is a verse that merits your lifetime of prayerful reflection: "How beautiful you are, how charming, my love, my delight" (7:7). From what you have discovered in prayerfully studying the New Testament and the constant teaching of the church, can you bring yourself to find in these words of the *Song* an accurate summary of how Jesus Christ regards you?

It is as if he, your bridegroom, contemplating your inner beauty, your virtues, your degree of passionate surrender to his guidance, sees in you as in a mirror his own beauty and perfections. You have been made according to his image and likeness (Gn 1:26). He is really the mirror in whom you see reflected your true, beautiful self in your transforming oneness with him: "They are the ones he chose specially long ago and intended to become true images of his Son" (Rom 8:29).

Yet Jesus looks at you and is thrilled at seeing his own beauty reflected in you who now have become for him a mirror in whom he discovers his own uniqueness in the love you have for him. The more you are united with him in perfect surrender, the more he can truly say within your heart: "How beautiful you are, how charming, my love, my delight."

Listen to St. Paul who should convince you that you are a mirror that reflects Jesus' perfections:

> And we, with our unveiled faces reflecting like mirrors the brightness of the Lord, all grow brighter and brighter as we are turned into the image that we reflect; this is the work of the Lord who is Spirit (2 Cor 3:18).

My Love, My Delight

1.   After the beloved has described in detail the beauty of his bride in all her physical parts, by way of summary he confesses that she is his love, his great delight. Overwhelmed that you should not only please Christ but that he should be thrilled and

delighted by your beautiful love for him, you may rightfully wonder how you bring him delight.

The concept of *delight* conveys the thought of gratifying or pleasing another greatly. It means to charm by bringing a high degree of pleasure, high satisfaction and joy to another. What a gift from the Holy Spirit to accept the truth that you have the power to delight the heart of Christ, your beloved! Yet how do you please him and give him joy? First, you recognize, as Mary realized, that it is God who has done great things to you. It is all his grace, his wonderful operations in your life that through the gifts of his Spirit have transformed you into a "new creation in Christ" (2 Cor 5:17).

Yet you have freely cooperated. You have decided to deny your false self, to take up the cross of suffering everything necessary in order to return his great love. You please Christ when you have put on his mind by an inner revolution (Eph 4:23) and live by his values. He is thrilled when he sees you joyfully accept and praise God for whatever sufferings come to you as you strive to live in love for him and your neighbor. The cross of Christ now is your delight and joy. The privilege of serving others humbles you. You are becoming his true image, his mirror in which he can discover himself living in your unique life of love, a new life he could not, in the same way, have lived on this earth. What joy you find in suffering, for you know bearing such trials out of love delights your beloved. More, more! Now the words of St. John the Baptist become your words also:

> The bride is only for the bridegroom;
> and yet the bridegroom's friend,
> who stands there and listens,
> is glad when he hears the bridegroom's voice.
> This same joy I feel, and how it is complete.
> He must grow greater,
> I must grow smaller.
> He who comes from above
> is above all others...(Jn 3:29-31).

Full Maturity

1. Psalm 92 describes the righteous as flourishing like palm trees

(Ps 92:12). Now the bridegroom by way of summarizing the beauty of his bride describes her spiritual maturity as a towering palm tree. "In stature like the palm tree, its fruit-clusters your breasts" (7:8). In her earlier development she had sought her beloved for what he could bring to her by way of consolations. She had not yet matured enough to bear the crosses and purifications he would send her. But now he is delighted by her maturity. Not only has she pushed her roots deep down in the desert of heat and dryness to touch the fountain of living waters, Christ, but, like the palm tree, in her maturity she brings forth great fruit.

Scripturally the palm tree is a sign of the Lord Jesus. Lifted up on the cross he has won the palm of victory. Now the bride is likened to the palm tree because she also has reached a oneness with him and stands straight and tall, unto the full maturity of the stature of Christ: "In this way we are all to come to unity in our faith and in our knowledge of the Son of God, until we become the perfect Man, fully mature with the fullness of Christ himself" (Eph 4:13).

2. The bride shows her maturity by her productivity. Not only is she united constantly with her beloved, but with his power within her she produces fruit in abundance for feeding others. She grows and is productive because she is united to Christ who gives her eternal life. With him in her she can bear all things. Although it is exposed to a hot desert climate, the palm tree's foliage and fruit all grow without hindrance because it is fed by a deep source of water.

Christ's bride lives in a desert where there is not much green life and much fruit brought forth. Yet, in spite of so many temptations around her, she grows because her source of growth and maturity is not from herself but from Christ.

3. The bride's breasts are compared to the huge fruit-clusters of the palm tree. A single large cluster of dates may produce over a thousand single dates and weigh 20 pounds or more. This image describes the capacity of the bride, united to Christ, to feed others. The breasts are not only an expression, as we saw earlier, of the love for God and neighbor, but they are also for the purpose of nursing the young. In her earlier immaturity the expression of love was more important. Now in her full maturity even

to the stature of Christ she has more capacity to nourish others.

The hungry come to her and through the fruit of the Spirit they see her from a far off, towering straight toward heaven. They are nourished through her example, her virtues, her teaching and counsel, but, above all, she pours out the love of Jesus from her inner source, from the deep roots that she has sunk into Christ, the core of her being.

Bearing Fruit in Plenty

1. The groom not only is ravished by his bride's beauty, but he now sees himself as the harvester of part of her beauty, namely, he comes to claim her fruit. When you have advanced to inner maturity and self-surrender, when you abide in him and he abides in you, Christ says to you: "Whoever remains in me, with me in him, bears fruit in plenty" (Jn 15:5). So in the *Song*: " 'I will climb the palm tree,' I resolved, 'I will seize its clusters of dates' " (7:9).

Part of Christ's delight in his bride is that he sees the fruit already ripe for the harvest like clusters of so many dates. Because the bride has climbed to great union with Christ, the palm tree of life, and there partaken of his precious fruits, she has now brought forth abundant fruit.

2. Christ gives an exhortation to his bride: "May your breasts be clusters of grapes, your breath sweet-scented as apples, your speaking, superlative wine" (7:9-10). These comparisons are all images that express the bride's fruitfulness toward others whom she lovingly nourishes by her virtuous acts of service.

Christ calls us, not only to live intimately in nuptial union with him, but also to fruitfulness in service toward others. With Christ in you, you are called with him to feed others. He prays here that the bride's breasts, which before were empty and unproductive, may now through his union with her become like clusters of grapes that produce wines that will intoxicate others with a love for Christ such as she has received from him. It is similar to Christ's prayer to his heavenly Father in the Last Supper discourse:

With me in them and you in me,

may they be so completely one
that the world will realize that it was you who sent me
and that I have loved them as much as you loved me
    (Jn 17:23).

3. Christ prays that his bride's breath be sweet-scented as apples. In chapter 2:3 the bridegroom is compared by the bride to
an apple tree in whose shade she sits and eats of his fruit, so sweet
to her taste. In Chapter 2:5, the bride prays that she be
strengthened and restored by his apples.Now Christ prays that
his beloved breathe upon others a fragrance as sweet as that of
apples. This comparison is in the context of Christ's prayerful wish
that his bride be productive and life-nourishing to others as he
has been to her.

A Superior Wine

1. The groom expresses a wish that his beloved possess a speech
toward others that is "a superlative wine." God's Word, Jesus
Christ, is preached and heard through his beloved disciples. How
can anyone hear and believe God's saving word unless persons
are sent to speak the word by their lives as examples that have
the quality to intoxicate others as good wine does?

The Bride Speaks

The Bride:

Wine flowing straight to my Beloved,
as it runs on the lips of those who sleep.
I am my Beloved's,
and his desire is for me.
Come, my Beloved,
let me go to the fields.
We will spend the night in the villages,
and in the morning we will go to the vineyards.
We will see if the vines are budding,
if their blossoms are opening,
if the pomegranate trees are in flower.
Then I shall give you

the gift of my love.
The mandrakes yield their fragrance,
the rarest fruits are at our doors;
the new as well as the old,
I have stored them for you, my Beloved (7:10-14).

Overflowing Wine

1.   The spouse, Christ, has praised the speech of his beloved as an excellent wine which gladens and intoxicates with joy the hearts of those who receive her words. The bride breaks in to confess humbly that such wine has to be traced directly to her beloved. "Wine flowing straight to my Beloved, as it runs on the lips of those who sleep" (7:10). She magnifies, as Mary does, her Lord and beloved, her spirit rejoices in God her Savior (Lk 1:46-47).

2.   Such intoxicating wine runs freely from "the lips of those who sleep." Sleep here refers to the bride and all other contemplatives who have entered into the mystical espousal with Christ as they now rest in his unifying love. They are asleep to the allurements of the world of illusions and deceits and are dynamically alive to Christ's words of truth. They rest in harmony and integration of body, soul and spirit as they experience their completion in Christ.

I Am My Beloved's

1.   The bride ecstatically cries out with boldness and certitude to bystanders: "I am my Beloved's, and his desire is for me" (7:11). She knows now, not by desire alone on her part, but from the praises given her by her spouse, that she belongs entirely to Christ and that he ardently desires her.

She is entering into the mystical marriage which brings such knowledge as only Christ's Spirit can give to her. On lower levels she, as we, wanted to be totally Christ's. She yearned that he would come and possess her as his own. But now there is an assured tone as she speaks to others that she belongs completely to him.

St. John of the Cross beautifully describes this entrance into the mystical marriage between the bride and Christ:

And I gave myself to Him,
Keeping nothing back;

In that sweet drink of God, in which the soul is im-
bibed in Him, she most willingly and with intense
delight surrenders herself wholly to him. In the desire
to be totally His and never to possess in herself
anything other than Him, God causes in this union the
purity and perfection necessary for such a surrender.
And since He transforms her in Himself, He makes her
entirely His own and empties her of all she possesses
other than Him.

   Hence, not only in her will but also in her works
she is really and totally given to God, without keeping anything back, just as God has freely given Himself
entirely to her. This union is so effected that the two
wills are mutually payed, surrendered, and satisfied
(so that neither fails the other in anything) with the
fidelity and stability of an espousal.[37]

There is now on two levels a breakthrough in the bride's
awareness. On the one hand, she has entered into a more perfect
love for her beloved. She loses her habitual sense of self which
before allowed her to consider herself as a self-contained entity,
independent and subjectively separable from Christ. Now, as St.
Teresa points out in the Seventh Mansion,[38] there is a forgetfulness
of self that is so complete that it seems the contemplative no longer
exists as an independently thinking person. She now lives totally
in every thought, word and action to glorify God. This is what
the bride means in her statement so full of complete surrender
of her selfhood as to find her happiness in living only for Christ:
"I am my Beloved's."

He Desires Me

   The other element of the new consciousness that comes to
the bride is how much her beloved truly loves her now and ardently desires to possess her. Most Christians in their earthly existence
never come to an awareness, experientially, of how much Christ,
who has died for each human person, truly and passionately

desires to love and be loved. Here we see the bride coming into this awareness that he *really* does want her. This is what constitutes the elements of a true marriage. Up to this point the Christian may believe Christ is God and, therefore, is loving out of his great perfections. He shows mercy to the sinful. He comes to save us by his condescending love.

But now the bride understands with great humility but, nonetheless, with certitude that Christ actually desires her for her own beauty. This awareness fills her with genuine humility, for she knows that all which is of beauty in her has come to her as gift from God. Yet there is also great joy for she knows that she has something of herself to offer that the bridegroom truly seeks with great desire. Such a belonging brings with this joy a peace and contentment at all times. This sense of oneness with the source of her being is manifested exteriorly on her countenance, in her walk, in her gestures and in her words to those around her. She has truly come home and possesses herself in her true self that cannot be any longer separated from Christ, whose image and likeness she has become.

This is the work of the Spirit, to give the bride of Christ the delight in the groom's passionate desire for her. Now there are no longer distinctions between pleasant and unpleasant happenings in her life. Everything is accepted with joy. Everything works unto good and unto the glory of her beloved. For no one can "unconvince" her of Christ's great desire for her at all times. And she eagerly embraces each moment and each event as the only place where he will come and desire her.

Come, My Beloved

1. Earlier on a lesser level of union with her beloved, the bride wanted to rest in the consolations of being alone with him. Now, aware of her oneness with him, it is she who invites her beloved, since she has now only one mind, that of his, to do what he always wishes to do, to go forth and bring forth fruit in great abundance so that others may enjoy a part of the abundant life he has come to give all. She is totally occupied now with helping him bring forth fruit in the lives of others. So it is with this understanding that she invites her spouse to go with her, not into her own garden

to enjoy intimacy with him, but to go out into the country, to go wherever people need both of them.

Now she has entered into a synthesis of the contemplative and the active life with no separation, for she is always not only in the presence of Christ, but she is worshipping the Father and loving his entire creation as she works with Christ to this end. Before, she experienced Christ working *in* her, but now he works *with* her. She lives in a *synergy*, a working with him, in and for him. Everything she does is prayer. As she rests in the oneness with her beloved that no one can take away from her, she is able to move out into the world of great multiplicity and diversity and never lose the inner "grounding" in him. And yet she is able with Christ to give herself completely to the moment and the work at hand as most important in building up the body of Christ. How often in the public life of Christ he summoned those who wished to follow him by his word: "Come." Now the bride, knowing full well the mind of Christ that she has put on, says it in anticipation of his invitation to her. For their union is to bring forth fruit in loving service that others may experience the same oneness with the groom. She invites him with the words: "Let us go to the fields" (7:12). The field is the world (Mt 13:38), but the bride no longer fears that the world will take her from her beloved. Before she found him only in her bed and garden, not in the city. Now she is no longer afraid, for she has heard in the depths of her heart his words: "Go, therefore, make disciples of all the nations; baptize them in the name of the Father and of the Son and of the Holy Spirit, and teach them to observe all the commands I gave you. And know that I am with you always; yes, to the end of time" (Mt 28:19-20).

A Night in the Villages

1.   "We will spend the night in the villages" (7:12). The bride has an expanded vision of reality. Now she is content to be anywhere in the world, so long as she is with Christ and working with and for him. She speaks of spending the night in the villages (plural) to indicate that she has no fixed abode she can call home. She is with Christ a pilgrim, detached from all securities, ready to pass the nights in any village throughout the world in order

to be of service with Christ for others. This is the type of celibacy that is of obligation on the part of all Christians who love Christ with all their hearts, whether they are living a marital or single or celibate life in terms of religious vows. They all are called to the same poverty of spirit or detachment to be sent by Christ wherever he wishes them to serve. Each style of life will manifest such detachment differently, as the individual Christian surrenders to find God's will in his or her free choices of that mode of serving God and neighbor.

Going to the Vineyards

1.   The bride is zealous to go with Christ into the vineyards to see what fruit is ready to be harvested: "...and in the morning we will go to the vineyards" (7:12). We should note that there are many vineyards mentioned by her. Earlier in Chapter 1:6, she confessed that her mother's sons made her look after the vineyards (in the plural), but she had not cultivated her own. She was immature in the spiritual life, was not united deeply with Christ, and did not submit completely to his inner directive voice, so she scattered her efforts in doing good, much to the neglect of her own spiritual growth and intimacy with Christ.

Now, grounded in a oneness with her beloved that nothing can take from her, she is able to go forth eagerly and with zest, "early in the morning" and engage all day long in apostolic works without neglecting her own spiritual union with Christ.

2.   We see that with deeper union with Christ, the Christian contemplative also puts on his mind and love for the whole world. Her interests are to think with the entire church (*Sentire cum ecclesia*) and to promote as far as she can, even if it is only by intercessory prayer, all works that build up the body of Christ. She may still "specialize" in one or other works within the vineyard of Christ, but her thinking has become "catholic," in the sense of extending her interests and efforts to embrace all activities in the church.

Spring—the Promise of Harvest

1.   What will she and her bridegroom do there in the vineyards? "We will see if the vines are budding, if their blossoms are open-

ing. If the pomegranate trees are in flower" (7:13). Christ has come to bring forth fruit, abundant life in his Father's creation. A grapevine is utterly useless if it does not produce fruit. It is fit only to be burned (Jn 15:6).

The House of Israel was the vineyard Yahweh planted and expected fruit from, but it produced none.

> Yes, the vineyard of Yahweh Sabaoth
> is the House of Israel,
> and the men of Judah
> that chosen plant.
> He expected justice, but found bloodshed,
> integrity, but only a cry of distress (Is 5:7).

Now both the bride and bridegroom come to the vineyard early in the morning, not only to see whether there is beginning life, a promise of a future harvest, but also to work there in the vineyard to cultivate what has already started to bring forth a promise of great harvest.

2. The pomegranate tree was used in Chapter 6:11 to indicate a fruit resembling the redemptive act of Christ dying on the cross and shedding his blood for the life of the world. Both lovers examine in the vineyard the pomegranate trees to see whether the fruits of Christ's passion and death are truly bearing fruit. The bride no longer sees her own fruit or work within the church but sees all works done for Christ, and she wishes to have a part, to help him bring forth fruit everywhere in all parts of the world, in all souls.

The Gift of Love

1. Then, in the active cultivation of the vineyards and other fruit-bearing trees, the bride confesses she will give to Christ the gift of her love: "Then I shall give you the gift of my love" (7:13). This indicated the degree of contemplation attained by the bride in her union with Christ. It is attained not in spite of her apostolic activities, but in her very giving of herself to others so that they might share the gift of Christ she has so abundantly received through deeper union in which she shows her love for her beloved. No longer is there a Martha in her working, overly anxious for

147

results while neglecting the Mary who sits at Christ's feet to contemplate him in utter rest and withdrawal from work. Now Martha and Mary have become the bride; work and contemplation are not separated. Love grows in every thought, word and deed.

She is nearing the permanent state of the mystical marriage with her spouse. We can see that it will not be something Christ does to her. Rather, it will be her continued awareness of what has always been true: that Christ lives within her in the most perfect, nuptial understanding. He is always giving himself unto death for love of her. But she must learn to give her love to him. As her giving to Christ becomes all-pervasive, as her love is more constant, she finds that she can always be united in her consciousness with him who is one with her. Nothing, no amount of activity, can take her away from her beloved. Everything about her and him is said in this phrase: "I shall give you the gift of my love" in all places, in all activities. The Spirit of love flows over her at all times. She is on fire with love for Christ. The more she loves the more she burns to love. As she discovers her union with Christ to continue and to increase through the very activities done out of love for him, she dares to do more, to pray more for the entire world, to be more available to all who come to her. She becomes compassion, like a universal mother to the entire, suffering world.

The Fragrance of Mandrakes

1.   The mandrake plant has a long history of being a powerful aphrodisiac to induce love and fertility in the female. It is a plant native to the Mediterranean area. We see it referred to in only one other place in scripture: the finding of the plants by Reuben in the wheat field. He presents them to his mother Leah who reluctantly gives them to Rachel so she might become fertile (Gn 30:14-16).

Co-workers With God

1.   The bride has changed radically from what she had been earlier. Then she was centered upon herself. The things she did for her beloved were exclusively hers, done in a realization that they belonged to her. She did them out of love for him but

totally with her own power. Now she understands that whatever she does of good and out of love is done with him and under his power. It is now "our" fruits at "our" doors. She also can appreciate the gifts and fruits brought forth by others to glorify her bridegroom. Even these fruits of others are considered "our" fruits. And so she beautifully expresses her new consciousness in these words: "The rarest fruits are at our doors: the new as well as the old, I have stored them for you, my Beloved" (7:14).

It is a great growth through purifications to arrive at such pure love that we can offer Christ our works and realize they are also his works, done in his Spirit of love. It is a continued growth to offer him also the works and fruits produced in the lives of others, of past times in the church and in the present, and rejoice in what they have done to build up the body of Christ. St. Paul well understood this oneness in the body of Christ, not only with him, the head, but also with all members working under the same Spirit for the same goal: to glorify God and build up the body of Christ, the church.

> Neither the planter nor the waterer matters: only God, who makes things grow. It is all one who does the planting and who does the watering, and each will duly be paid according to his share in the work. We are fellow workers with God: you are God's farm, God's building (1 Cor 3:7-9).

In true love for Christ, the members no longer feel any spirit of competition or jealousy toward others in the same body of Christ. For they know with St. Paul that "There is a variety of gifts but always the same Spirit; there are all sorts of service to be done, but always to the same Lord; working in all sorts of different ways in different people, it is the same God who is working in all of them. The particular way in which the Spirit is given to each person is for a good purpose" (1 Cor 12:4-7).

2. The bride refers to fruits both new and old. These could refer to the new enlightenment of her oneness with the entire body of Christ and her awareness of oneness with the saints of the church who have produced rare fruits in earlier times and are still present in the church through their examples and intercessory prayers.

Their fruits are the "old" that still build up the body of Christ. Those living now are producing new fruits that build upon the fruits of former holy members of Christ.

3. The new and the old fruits can also refer to the bride's integration within her own life. She wishes to do all for love of Christ, her beloved. The *old* can refer to all thoughts, words and deeds that flow out from her human nature. She wishes all to be permeated by her transcendent love from the Spirit so that everything be a growing in greater love for Christ: "Whatever you eat, whatever you drink, whatever you do at all, do it for the glory of God" (1 Cor 10:31). The *new* indicates the fruit she brings forth through her insertion into Christ as now constituting a "new creation" (2 Cor 5:17). She wishes that all of her life be lifted up by the leaven of her beloved living within her and operating through his Spirit to make everything fruitful by permeating it with love.

All these she brings together as storing them up, for such acts and thoughts done out of love truly transform her into love. She no longer presents to him things she has done, but a loving person who has become conscious love for her beloved, whom she is so fond of calling her groom. She now knows he passionately loves her and desires to possess her completely as his own.

Chapter Eight

The Bride:

Ah, why are you not my brother,
nursed at my mother's breast!
Then if I met you out of doors, I could kiss you
without people thinking ill of me.
I should lead you, I should take you
into my mother's house, and you would teach me!
I should give you spiced wine to drink,
juice of my pomegranates.

His left arm is under my head
and his right embraces me.

The Bridegroom:

I charge you,
daughters of Jerusalem,
not to stir my love, nor rouse it,
until it please to awake (8:1-4).

My Brother

1. The bride, almost beside herself with ecstatic love for her bridegroom, pours out her love and her passionate desire for greater loving union with him in terms that fit no logical categories or understanding. She would lovingly wish that he would be her little brother, a baby still nursed at her mother's breast, so that she could freely in public demonstrate her love for him at all times. In ancient Israel it was totally unacceptable to kiss publicly, even for a husband and wife, let alone espoused lovers. Yet it was acceptable for blood relatives, such as brother and sister, to do so. The bride is complaining that the intimacy she experiences for her beloved when she is alone with him in total, loving absorption cannot be experienced or demonstrated publicly before the eyes of others. They would be shocked to hear the wild demonstrations of love that she bestows upon him when they are alone. Yet how she would wish she could do so at all times without any restraint, for she has now reached that state of being so totally one with him that she would wish to let others also see that oneness.

What a pain for those who have reached such union with Christ to want to witness to the whole world how beautiful is their bridegroom! And yet how little of such intimate, loving sighs, heroic protests of fidelity, and readiness to die for him would others who do not enjoy a similar state of oneness with him understand?

2. Such souls know also, in this complaint of the bride, what pain it is to remain in the confinement of bodily existence, not to be freed from such restraint imposed on their loving union with Christ. This is the loving complaint that St. Paul wrote of to the Philippians:

I am caught in this dilemma: I want to be gone and be with Christ, which would be very much the better, but for me to stay alive in this body is a more urgent need for your sake. This weighs with me so much that I feel sure I shall survive and stay with you all, and help you to progress in the faith and even increase your joy in it; and so you will have another reason to give praise to Christ Jesus on my account when I am with you again (Phil 1:23-26).

Contemplatives who have experienced such mystical union with Christ would want always to stay on that same level of consciousness. Yet they are now, unlike the bride earlier, ready to give themselves in labors to help others to know and love their beloved, even if it means lessening their consolations. Still, this verse seems to say, such persons would wish that those whom they serve would already be on such a level of perfection that all would be able to share such intimacies in the company of one another, as will happen in heaven.

Teach Me

1. The bride in a playful mood tells her beloved: "I should lead you, I should take you into my mother's house, and you would teach me!" (8:2). The mother of the bride is the church where she was born into Christ's life. It was there she was begotten by his Spirit into a new life, where she was "born from above" (Jn 3:3), born "through water and the Spirit" (Jn 3:5). It is there she wishes still more to be taught by Christ the intimate mysteries of his great love for her and for the world.

This phrase concerning the bride's being taught by the groom has eschatological references to texts in the Old Testament where Yahweh would instruct his people, such as in Isaiah 48:17; 54:13; 55:1 ff and Jeremiah 31:33-34. In the Christian East Christ has always been called *Hagia Sophia*, Holy Wisdom. He says to all who wish to receive his true wisdom:

"Come and eat my bread,
drink the wine I have prepared!
Leave your folly and you will live,
walk in the ways of perception" (Prv 9:5-6).

How appropriate that the bride who is entering into the most intimate stage of union with Christ should speak in such terms of complete and final enlightenment, which only Christ can give. Such knowledge becomes the same as loving union; *gnosis* (knowing) becomes *agape* (perfect love).

Intoxicating Wisdom

1. The bride is praying here for the fullest of wisdom or experiential knowledge of God's divine love for her in the person of the Incarnate Word, Jesus Christ. She says: "I should give you spiced wine to drink, juice of my pomegranates" (8:2). She is coming into the mystical marriage where she will be able to give to her beloved, Christ, what he has been giving to her. She wishes to give him wine that is spiced. Wine was spiced to give both delightful taste and aroma. She has received this intoxicating, sweet-smelling wine from her Savior through his Spirit. She has drunk deeply of this wine and has come now to know the mysteries of God's tender and passionate love for her in giving her his Son, Jesus Christ. Through his teachings she has come to a transforming knowledge. She has been lifted up to be an exhilarating, intoxicating love to Christ, and now she is offering to give herself completely to him as he has given himself to her.

2. She offers him the juice of her pomegranates. Human language is so inadequate to express what the mystical marriage means except for those who have experienced that mutual exchange. St. John of the Cross explains that

> the pomegranates stand for the mysteries of Christ, the judgments of the wisdom of God, and the virtues and attributes uncovered in the knowledge of these innumerable mysteries and judgments. Just as pomegranates have many little seeds, formed and sustained within the circular shell, so each of the attributes, mysteries, judgments and virtues of God, like a round shell of power and mystery, holds and sustains a multitude of marvelous decrees and wondrous effects.[39]

Through the Holy Spirit she has drunk of the juice of the

many attributes of Christ's personality, his divinity and humanity, of all that is written about his beauty and love in the gospels. This amazing love of the God-man has transformed her from sterility into fertility and given her the power now to bring forth his very own life-giving love. She is now offering that love of equality, the completely gratuitous, transforming gift of God's Spirit of love that yet allows her to realize she is a gift desired by Christ. All human beings, hopefully, in at least their deepest human loves, have experienced in shadowy form what the bride is experiencing now in her mystical oneness in marriage with Christ. But how can human language express this mystery of all mysteries?

The next verse is a simple description of that mystical marriage with Christ. The bride knows she will be able to give him back the juice of his pomegranates, and still it will be her unique gift also. Her loving acts, which now resemble his and still are in some way his yet also in a very real sense her own, will delight the bridegroom in a new way. His own love does not thrill his heart until it comes back to him in her surrendering love.

The Mystical Marriage

1. The bride had spoken the words of this verse earlier; but now she understands them in the new and more mystical way of complete surrender to her beloved: "His left arm is under my head and his right embraces me" (8:3). In Chapter 2:6 he brought her into the banqueting house. Now she has brought him into her mother's house. Both scenes evoke a wedding banquet and all the joys and happiness that accompany such a festivity. Now in a new consummation of her earlier espousal to Christ, the bride-contemplative experiences Christ taking over completely as she totally surrenders to the gift of himself. She understands the scriptural text that describes the almighty hand of God supporting her head:

> The God of old, he is your refuge.
> Here below, he is the age-old arm
> driving the enemy before you... (Dt 33:27).

Now she knows a new, all-encompassing support of Christ

154

in her life; no trial or tribulation can ever separate her from his love.

> Nothing therefore can come between us and the love of Christ, even if we are troubled or worried, or being persecuted, or lacking food or clothes, or being threatened or even attacked....These are the trials through which we triumph, by the power of him who loved us. For I am certain of this: neither death nor life, no angel, no prince, nothing that exists, nothing still to come, not any power, or height or depth, nor any created thing, can ever come between us and the love of God made visible in Christ Jesus our Lord (Rom 8:35-39).

Christ supports the bride's head, the source of her intellect. She is now convinced that she has entered into a union with Christ that allows her to abandon herself, in every thought, desire and image, to his strength. He will make it up with his wisdom, as St. James says: "If there is any one of you who needs wisdom, he must ask God, who gives to all freely and ungrudgingly; it will be given to him" (Jas 1:5). She is totally of one mind with Christ. Now it is as if she had no mind of her own. Her consciousness is informed constantly by the consciousness of Christ. She can no longer think of herself as living or having any existence outside of Christ. She understands now what it means that God created her according to the image and likeness of his Word, Jesus Christ.

2. Now she experiences how Christ's right hand embraces her. He holds her in loving embrace so she can always look upon his face as she touches so closely his heart. God's right hand is for her defense; throughout scripture such an allusion refers to God's strength and protection toward his loved ones. In this text the image of the right hand of Christ not only describes his protective love against all inimical forces (Ps 17:8), but it also hints at the ecstatic joys and consolations the bride now receives as she enters into this final stage of mystical oneness with Christ in full marriage. She is overwhelmed with the power of Christ's Spirit that shoots through her and burns up any last resistance to full

union with him. She understands now what a privilege it was to have suffered any trials or purifications in order to enter into such a hundredfold of ecstatic union (Mt 19:23).

Do Not Awaken Her

1.   Two times the bridegroom leads his beloved to a new level of oneness and bids the daughters of Jerusalem who stand around the bride not to stir her (2:7; 3:5). The divine spouse leads his bride first away from any attachment to the senses, especially from an overweening desire for sense consolations in prayer. This comes about by trials of aridity and seeming absences of the groom, along with a sense of her unworthiness and betrayal of Christ through selfishness.

The second sleep comes after she has been thoroughly purified in both senses and spirit and enters into a more perfect oneness with him that assures her she is espoused to him forever. Now, in this third level of mystical union with Christ, the bride has become aware of her belonging to him forever in marital oneness. No one can stir her or take this union away from her. She needs this period of resting in the new-found, union that makes all other breakthroughs seem like so much darkness compared to high noon. This rest is important, for this level of ecstatic, loving oneness with her beloved needs to permeate every atom of her being. Out of this rest there will come forth a new energy. Her life will now be a *synergy*, a working with Christ, a true *symbiosis*, a life that is Christ's very own life in her. No longer will she act on her own, nor have any thought or idea that is not consciously rooted in Christ's wisdom. She alone will awake herself and return to share this love with others. She will go forth, no longer out of vanity or spiritual pride, but humbly and joyfully, to serve others as the lowliest of all handmaids of the Lord.

Conclusion

(8:5-7)

The Chorus:

> Who is this coming up from the desert
> leaning on her beloved?

The Bridegroom:

> I awakened you under the apple tree,
> there where your mother conceived you,
> there where she who gave birth to you conceived you.

> Set me like a seal on your heart,
> like a seal on your arm.
> For love is strong as Death,
> jealousy relentless as Sheol.
> The flash of it is a flash of fire,
> a flame of Yahweh himself.
> Love no flood can quench,
> no torrents drown (8·5-7)

Up From the Desert

1.   The final section of the *Song* serves as a summation of all that went before. The chorus sets the scene whereby the story of the bride and the bridegroom comes to an ending. Once before, not the chorus of the daughters of Jerusalem, but the bridegroom himself had asked in wonderment: "What is this coming up from the desert like a column of smoke?" (3:6). This was spoken at the beginning of the bride's intimate union with her beloved. She went into the desert to renounce her self-centeredness as she fought the interior battles necessary to live more completely for the Lord.

157

The chorus is surprised at the great change the daughters of Jerusalem now see in the bride who comes out of the desert leaning on her beloved.

There are two deserts that all who wish to follow Christ must enter into and do the spiritual battles necessary in order to come out of them transformed. The first kind of desert wandering is in that particular desert that carries our own name. You have your desert and I have mine. It consists of all the brokenness and bias toward the false ego that come into our genes by birth and into our consciousness through education and social intercourse with the world around us. The causes are numerous; the effect is always the same—selfishness that lives in separation, and not love toward God and neighbor. The bride has entered into that darkened desert, and there Christ became her divine physician. There she learned through weeping and mourning, through calling on his name that he comes and helps her in her weakness. She comes out now with her acquired spiritual poverty, possessing the kingdom of heaven (Mt 5:3).

She is beautifully described as leaning upon Christ in her weakness. She is worn out because of her labors and has no more strength to wander about under her own power or according to her wishes. Her wandering, as that of the Israelites in the desert, has gone on for a long time, but now she leaves it. Christ is her sole support.

2. The other desert is that of the world around the bride, and this is something exterior to her from which she cannot escape. Trials and purifications will always come from this desert. She has entered into the kingdom of God but she remains in pilgrimage. She is already in Christ, but the world around her knows him not and will always treat her with scorn and persecute her because, as Jesus prophesied, "They will do these things because they have never known either the Father or myself" (Jn 16:3). But the message is clear. She leans upon her beloved as her strength and sole support. Her life is totally lived in him. She has no eyes for worldly pleasures to satisfy herself, nor does she fear the evil forces that come from such worldliness.

She has heard the words of St. Paul and has come out of

her inner desert to enter into a vision of reality that can bear the worldly desert around her.

> Since you have been brought back to true life with Christ, you must look for the things that are in heaven, where Christ is, sitting at God's right hand. Let your thoughts be on heavenly things, not on the things that are on the earth, because you have died, and now the life you have is hidden with Christ in God. But when Christ is revealed — and he is your life—you too will be revealed in all your glory with him (Col 3:1-4).

Under the Apple Tree

1. The bridegroom tells his bride that it is under the apple tree, which they apparently are passing by, that he awakened her. In many literary traditions the apple tree is referred to as an erotic symbol, a place where lovers meet and enter into loving intimacy with each other. The bride earlier referred to her beloved as the apple tree, more beautiful than all other beings (2:3). She first awakened under his love to realize that only he could possess her heart since his love was superior to that of all other beings. She found sustenance and security in the shade of his love.

Now she realizes in a more complete way that Christ wins her love by dying on the wood of the cross. It is this deeper realization of Christ's burning love for her through his death on the cross that becomes the transforming power to heal her of her "unredeemed" self and make her worthy to become his true bride.

New Awakening

2. Christ, by the mystery of his death on the cross and his resurrection which permits him to release his Spirit into his bride's heart, is able to "regenerate" her into a new creation (2 Cor 5:17; 1 Jn 5:1). He notes that he awakens her under the same tree where the mother of the bride first conceived her and there brought her forth in birth (8:5). This mother is Eve who conceived all of us in sin under the forbidden tree in the Garden of Eden. She gave birth to us in our carnal, fleshly selves under the sign of that tree of shame.

The bride is awakened by Christ first to see her fallen nature

159

and her total inability to save herself. Christ then leads her into the inner knowledge that it is solely through him that she can be restored to the beauty and dignity to which the heavenly father destined her when he predestined her in Christ Jesus. God raised her up when she lay dead in her sleep (Eph 2:1) all because of what Christ on the cross did to heal her. Salvation is God's pure gift, not anything she could do (Eph 2:5-8).

A Seal on God's Heart

1.   The bride is overcome with humility at being reminded by her beloved of her inability by her own power to be beautiful and loving in response to his great love. Yet she thrills with purer love for Christ as she realizes his ever-abiding presence that makes it possible for her to be his true love.

Christ continues to exhort her now to abide in his perfect love. How beautifully the Spirit expresses this in the phrase: "Set me like a seal on your heart, like a seal on your arm" (8:6). A seal in the ancient Near East, when unbroken on letters, on legal and official documents or on a tomb, guaranteed the authenticity of the contents. But it also indicated ownership, such as storage jar handles stamped with the seal of the owner. A seal, therefore, was like one's legal signature and sign of identification.

Pharaoh gave his signet ring to Joseph to empower him to act as his royal deputy. Yahweh made a solemn promise to elect and exalt Zerubbabel and his tribe from which Christ would come: "When that day comes—it is Yahweh Sabaoth who speaks—I will take you, Zerubbabel son of Shealtiel, my servant—it is Yahweh Sabaoth who speaks—and make you like a signet ring. For I have chosen you—it is Yahweh Sabaoth who speaks" (Hg 2:23).

In this verse Christ is asking you, his bride, to set him like a seal on your heart. In substance he is always asking you to take him as your perfect beloved and to prefer no one else to him: "As my heavenly Father created you with the stamp and image of me upon your soul, now I ask you to place me in your consciousness as the only one to whom you lovingly belong. I have purchased you from slavery to sin by my blood. But now I seek your free gift. My imageness in you cannot reach full likeness unless you choose to place me as a seal on your heart. Only you can witness

by your life of prayer, by your virtuous acts, by the gifts of my
Holy Spirit, that you belong totally to me as I have always been
totally your beloved."

A Seal on the Arm

1.   Christ asks that the bride place him as a seal on her arm. *Arm*
here could refer poetically to the hand and, therefore, to the realm
of strength and doing. Note in prophecy how Christ has carved
your name in the palms of his hands, when he was pierced by
nails on the cross for your sake (Is 49:16). If you bear Christ as
a seal in your heart and in your hands, all your thoughts, words
and deeds will bear his likeness. If you belong entirely to Christ
by bearing his stamp, you consciously will want to live lovingly
for him in all you are and do.

True love is proved by deeds. By this, Christ tells you, others
will know you are "my bride," if you love others as he has loved
you (Jn 15:12-17). Faith in him begets a return in love. But love
without works is dead (Jas 2:26).

Love—Strong as Death

1.   The groom seeks to describe to his bride how great is his love
for her. He personifies Love and compares it to Death in all its
fierce power. We know how great is the power of death over all
that lives! No one can plead and persuade death to spare a loved
one claimed by it. No money can buy more time from death. No
bargains can be struck. Death mocks our futile attempts to overcome its power. For death will be the victor.

Yet Christ's love for his bride is equally as strong. He has
loved her with a love that went beyond the power of death. No
greater love could he have than to lay down his life for His bride
(Jn 15:13). She was ever before his eyes and, therefore, "Let us
not lose sight of Jesus, who leads us in our faith and brings it to
perfection: for the sake of the joy which was still in the future,
he endured the cross, disregarding the shamefulness of it, and from
now on has taken his place at the right of God's throne" (Heb
12:2).

Before Christ's coming God's love was an equal match for
death. But Christ's death and resurrection have conquered over

the powers of death. Now death is swallowed up in victory. Death, you no longer are as strong as God's love. You have no victory, you have no sting (1 Cor 15:54-55). Christ holds the keys over your kingdom of darkness (Rv 1:18).

How great and immeasurable is Christ's love for you, because it is also the imaged and perfect love of the Father: "As the Father loves me, so I love you" (Jn 15:9).

A Jealous Love

1. Scripture describes God as a *jealous* lover: "For I, Yahweh your God, am a jealous God and I punish the father's fault in the sons...of those who hate me, but I show kindness to thousands of those who love me and keep my commandments" (Ex 20:5-6). St. Paul also describes his own love for his faithful as sharing in God's jealous love: "You see, the jealousy that I feel for you is God's own jealousy" (2 Cor 11:2).

The groom seeks again to describe how passionate and everlasting is his love for his bride by contrasting his love as a "jealousy relentless as Sheol" (8:6). If we stress the *passionate* aspect of the word *jealousy*, we would come closer to an understanding of Christ's burning, obdurate, everlasting love for his bride. Hell will never give up its citizens, nor will Christ, with a similar tenacity, ever give up loving his beloved.

How strengthened you should be in his everlasting love! Such love is to beget a similar love in your heart for him, so that you will willingly bear all trials and sufferings because, by his Spirit, your love also is passionate and fierce as Sheol.

A Flash of Fire

1. Love is described by the groom as "a flash of fire" (8:6). Periodically during his public life the love of Jesus for his Father and for all of us human beings flamed out in flashes of new and ardent longing: "I have come to bring fire to the earth and how I wish it were blazing already! There is a baptism I must still receive and how great is my distress till it is over!" (Lk 12:49-50). His baptism in the Spirit of the Father's love would be of water and blood poured out from his loving heart, the heart of a suffering God, imaged in Jesus.

When the spear would open his heart and release the last drops of water and blood, Jesus' work would be consummated: "It is accomplished" (Jn 19:30). God in man has now finally spoken his definitive word in Jesus Christ. The horrendous folly of the sufferings of Christ is sheer nonsense except in terms of the logic of divine love!

Yet Christ's love becomes a constant "flash of love" as he continually sends down his Spirit. His first disciples received the outpouring of the Spirit's love as flaming tongues of fire that stood over the heads of the disciples (Acts 2:3).

A Flame of Yahweh

1. The mystery of the Holy Spirit is that he is a flame of the Trinity's love for each of us. This flame is sent by the Father and the Son as a sharing in their burning love for each other—a love experienced only through the personalized Spirit of love. The greatest happiness you and I can possess is to become increasingly aware of this burning love of the Trinity dwelling within us at all times. This "flame of Yahweh" enkindles within us a burning love for the Trinity and for all God's creatures. This flame of the Holy Spirit cauterizes and burns out all remnants of selfishness in us. It transfigures us into a flaming light of knowledge and understanding, but, above all, of love. We become "divinized" as we become a flame of God's love toward all others.

2. St. John of the Cross beautifully expresses how this flame of God's love is the Holy Spirit:

> This flame of love is the Spirit of its Bridegroom, which is the Holy Spirit. The soul feels Him within itself not only as a fire which has consumed and transformed it, but as a fire that burns and flares within it....And that flame, every time it flares up, bathes the soul in glory and refreshes it with the quality of divine life. Such is the activity of the Holy Spirit in the soul transformed in love: the interior acts He produces shoot up flames for they are acts of inflamed love, in which the will of the soul united with that flame, made one with it, loves most sublimely.[40]

The bride of Christ has reached the mystical oneness with him. No longer does she experience Jesus as an object, loving her from the outside. Now day and night she is aware that she has become fire, as he is fire. She cannot determine where her fire ends and his begins. He so completely penetrates every atom of her being that she is fire and he is fire. There is only fire! She has become transformed into Christ by the love of the Spirit.

St. Symeon the New Theologian (+ 1022), Byzantine mystic of Constantinople, expresses this mysticism of fire and light:

> But, O what intoxication of light, O what movements
>   of fire!
> O, what swirlings of the flame in me, miserable
>   one that I am,
>   coming from you and Your glory!
> The glory I know it and I say it is Your Holy Spirit,
> who has the same nature with You and the same
>   honor, O Word;
> He is of the same race, of the same glory,
> of the same essence, He alone with Your Father
> and with You, O Christ, O God of the universe
> I fall down in adoration before You.
> I thank You that You have made me worthy
>   to know, however little it may be,
>   the power of Your divinity.
> I thank you that You, even when I was
>   sitting in darkness,
> revealed Yourself to me, You enlightened me,
> You granted me to see the light of your countenance
>   that is unbearable to all.
> I remained seated in the middle of darkness,
>   I know,
> but, while I was there surrounded by darkness,
> You appeared as light, illuminating
>   me completely from Your total light.
> And I became light in the night, I who was found
>   in the midst of darkness.[41]

No Flood Can Quench

1. Water is seen often in the bible as an image of the abode of Death. It depicts any destructive power against life and its full

enjoyment. The prophet Jonah prays a prayer of thanksgiving for deliverance from the waters that engulfed him:

> Out of my distress I cried to Yahweh
> and he answered me;
> from the belly of Sheol I cried,
> and you have heard my voice...
> And I said: I am cast out
> from your sight....
> The waters surrounded me right to my throat
> (John 2:3,5,6).

This verse: "Love no flood can quench, no torrents drown" (8:7) is saying more than that love is a fire that cannot be extinguished by water. Love is a force that all the mighty waters of the great deep and its rivers cannot overcome. Love withstands all forces of Death. No waters of trials and tribulations, no enemies of any kind, can ever conquer and subdue such a divine love given to the bride.

In a more positive way it says that one like the bride, who has tasted such divine love, despises all things, is ready to bear all things, to lose everything in order to have this pearl of great price. Having such love, for with St. Paul, she considers all else as mere rubbish in order to possess this love of Christ:

> For him I have accepted the loss of everything, and I look on everything...as so much rubbish if only I can have Christ and be given a place in him.... All I want is to know Christ and the power of his resurrection and to share his sufferings by reproducing the pattern of his death (Phil 3:8,10).

The End is the Beginning

This is the way that the *Song of Songs* ends.[42] The final words in this powerful love song of God's passionate longing, both for his people, Israel, and the church of Christ, and for each individual member who belongs to the *ekklesia* or "called-out" people of God, are rightfully spoken by the bridegroom. The emphasis is no longer on the bride in her cries of piercing, wounding love for her beloved: "I am my Beloved's, and my Beloved is mine" (6:3).

God's love song is completed, yet always wondrously there is a new beginning with the words of Christ addressed now and always to you and me individually, and, therefore, to his people, the fulfilled church of Christ.

Christ's love is a fire, the same flame of the Father, but now experienced by the bride through the lasting kiss of the Holy Spirit. He promises to be present in love outpoured for you. No obstacle can overcome the force of such a burning love. No waters can extinguish this flaming fire of love that Christ has for you.

A Life in Christ

You have broken through the world of objectivity and have entered into a union with Christ that becomes so real and yet so utterly inexplicable by you to others who have not received such an experience of oneness. You live consistently on this level of union with Christ, an experience described by St. Paul when he wrote: "Anyone who is joined to the Lord is one spirit with him" (1 Cor 6:17). You yearn to be dissolved and to be even more one with Christ, yet you are content to serve him by bringing him to others: "Life to me, of course, is Christ, but then death would bring me something more" (Phil 1:21).

Christ Everywhere

You have been swept up into the marital union with Christ so that you now habitually experience the presence powerfully and peacefully at the core of your being. This presence moves out of you, but takes you along in loving service to the world around you. In other human beings you find the same Christ, laughing in the joyful, suffering in those who are heavy-burdened. This oneness with Christ and the human scene is well described by Caryll Houselander in her own "mystical" oneness with Christ in a London subway:

> I was in an underground train, a crowded train in which all sorts of people jostled together, sitting and strap-hanging-workers of every description going home at the end of the day. Quite suddenly I saw with my mind, but as vividly as a wonderful picture, Christ in them all. But I saw more than that: not only was

Christ in every one of them, living in them, dying in them, rejoicing in them, sorrowing in them—but because He was in them, and because they were here the whole world was here too, here in this underground train; not only the world as it was at that moment, not only all the people in all the countries of the world, but all those people who had lived in the past, and all those yet to come. I came out into the street, and walked for a long time in the crowds. It was the same here, on every side, in every passer-by, everywhere—Christ....[43]

As you have entered into the oneness of the lights of two candles, as St. Teresa of Avila describes the mystical marriage,[44] you find that you are one with Christ as "the wicks and the wax and the light are all one." You are in the image and likeness of Christ. But now you know too that each human being has also been made according to Christ for such a union. And you go forth with zeal to help to restore each human person you are privileged to meet and serve according to the same image and likeness of Christ. The more defaced is that image in any human being you meet, the more ardently you strive to help to recreate it, so that Jesus Christ again shines forth in all his divine splendor latent in each person. You wish, in great love and responsibility, to serve your neighbor with an active love that will smooth away lines of fear and grief and consternation on the faces of human beings. You rejoice, too, when Jesus Christ, the eternal youth, conquers the heart of one other human being in order to bring forth joy and happiness in the world.

The Active Contemplative

"The end of the ages" (1 Cor 10:11) has come upon you. God has taken a piece of this imperfect world, you in all your creatureliness and broken humanity, and has transfigured it into his glorious, risen Son. But you believe also that the same power within you (1 Jn 4:4) can be released through your cooperation in the struggling world around you. He continues to transform creation into a new Jerusalem. Jesus, the high-priest, is still breathing over the groaning world to transfigure raw matter into a Spirit-filled cosmos.

As Jesus, in history, needed the contemplative, Mary, to receive him into her very being through the power of the Holy Spirit, and then to be given as the life to the world, so he needs you and other human beings to "beget" him again, to render him "enfleshed" into a world that lies in darkness. The end of the *Song* is not to rest in ecstatic union with your bride, but it is for you to become a *mother* of your beloved. You, the bride, are to become the mother of the bridegroom! Unheard of miracle! how beautifully did Meister Eckhart, the 14th-century Rhenish Dominican mystic, express this archetypal symbol of fruitful woman in all human beings in these bold words:

> For man to become fruitful, he must become a woman. Woman! That is the most noble word that can be addressed to the soul, and it is far nobler than virgin. That man should conceive God within himself is good and in this predisposition he is a virgin. But that God should become fruitful in him is better. For to become fruitful through the gift received is to be grateful for the gift. And then the intellect becomes a woman in its gratitude that conceives anew.

No longer do you move through this world seeking to do all your "works" in a contemplative atmosphere but, rather, now you, as Christ's bride, always one with him, do all things in him with his very strength united to yours, to being forth, to call into a birthing, new Christ-life in yourself, around yourself, and within the lives of those around you. Contemplation flows from the fullness of your activities, since you find Christ in the very activity. You discover the community of your *I-Thou* in Christ's Spirit, uniting both you and Christ to the Father. You find the Holy Trinity at work in the most commonplace action.

You no longer strive to be recollected by removing yourself consciously from the pressing of the crowds and the wild, hectic movements around you. Yours is now a recollection by which you are absorbed in God and at the same time very much aware of the crowd, since you see in each one in that crowd a brother and sister in Christ, actually or in potency through grace. You see on each one the mark of the sacred blood of Jesus Christ, his burning love, as you have come to experience that love for you personally. For you there can be no insignificant event that does not bear the stamp of the Holy Trinity's desire to redeem all creation and restore it through Christ to the original plan as conceived by the Holy Trinity.

Whatever you do by way of work, you contemplate the Trinity. Your action proceeds precisely from your centering upon Christ, as the source of your being and that of the world's being in the Word of God. The community in Christ, your spouse, opens you out into the trinitarian community. The many are in the one, the one is in the many. God is community and it is love, emptying love that unites and yet calls out the uniqueness of each other in the oneness. Christ's presence within you is a light that is seen stretching outwards and always upwards. The apostles "looked up" and saw Jesus Christ and Moses and Elijah transfigured on top of Mount Tabor. The movement of a person of deep prayer is from darkness toward the transcendent light of God's presence everywhere. From unreality to reality, from darkness to light, from non-Christ to Christ, from bride of Christ to mother of Christ!

The message of the *Song* when seen in its fullest meaning in Christ ends in a similar way to the conclusion of the Book of Revelation:

The throne of God and of the Lamb
will be in its place in the city:
his servants will worship him,
they will see him face to face,
and his name will be written on their foreheads.
It will never be night again
and they will not need lamplight or sunlight,
because the Lord God will be shining on them.
They will reign for ever and ever (Rv 22:3-5)

FOOTNOTES

Introduction

1. Cited by Marvin H. Pope: *Song of Songs; A New Translation with Introduction and Commentary, The Anchor Bible Series* (Garden City, N.Y.: Doubleday & Company, Inc., 1977), p. 89.

2. Two works that have presented a survey of the major schools of interpretation are John Bradley White; *A Study of the Language of Love in the Song of Songs and Ancient Egyptian Poetry* (Missoul, MT: Scholars Press, 1978) and Hugh J. Schonfield, *The Song of Songs* (London: Elek Bks. Ltd., 1959). Cf. also the rather extension survey given by Marvin H. Pope: op.cit.; pp. 89-229.

3. Augustinus Bea, S.J.: *Canticum Canticorum Salamonis* (Rome: Scripta Pontifici Istituti Biblici, 1953) no. 104.

4. Gregory of Nyssa: *The Life of Moses* trans. Abrahan J. Malherbe and Everett Ferguson in the series: *The Classics of Western Spirituality* (Ramsey, N.J.: Paulist Press, 1978).

5. St. Bernard: *Sermons on the Canticles*, Sermon 79, *PL*: Vol. 183 (Paris: Migne, 1879) no. 1; 1163 B—C.

Text

1. All quotes taken from the works of St. John of the Cross are from the edition: *The Collected Works of St. John of the Cross*, trans. Kieran Kavanaugh, O.C.D., and Otilio Rodriguez, O.C.D. (Washington D.C.: ICS Publications, 2131 Lincoln Road, N.E. 20002, 1979). This quote is found on p. 411.

2.   Bernard of Clairvaux: *On the Song of Songs I* (Spencer, MA: Cistercian Publications, 1971) Sermon 8, pp. 45-52; trans Kilian Walsh, O.C.S.O.

3.   Ibid. *Sermon* 8:7, p. 51.

4.   Pseudo-Augustine: *Soliloquies,* Bk. 1, Ch 30 *PL* 40, 888.

5.   St. Bernard: op.cit., Sermon 23, pp. 19-20, Sermon 4,1, p. 22.

6.   The Septuagint translation from Hebrew to Greek and St. Jerome's Vulgate version from Greek to Latin has for "your love" the translation, "your breasts." Recent scholars are agreed that this appears to be a mistake, although there are grounds for the choice since the words *dodim* in Hebrew means "love(s)" and *daddayim* means "breasts" or "teats" and appeared the same in the ancient consonantal orthography "*ddm.*" In this verse "your love(s)" is preferred from the context to "your breasts" since the female is speaking about and to the male. For a detailed account of this passage, cf.*The Anchor Bible: Song of Songs,* intro. and commentary by Marvin H. Pope (Garden City, N.Y.: Doubleday & Company, Inc., 1977) p. 298.

7.   The word in Hebrew, "alamot," implies the idea of young girls of adolescent age. Thus many Fathers took this suggestion of youth and vigor to refer to those reborn in baptism and who have had their youth renewed like eagles, as St. Ambrose and St. Gregory the Great interpret it. St. Bernard is representative of the medieval commentators as he writes: "But the maidens have less understanding and therefore less knowledge. They are not well-equipped to penetrate sublime truths. Still infants in Christ, they must be fed with milk and oil." Op.cit., *Sermon* 19, 7; p. 144.

8.   Origen: *The Song of Songs,* trans. R.P. Lawson, in Ancient Christian Writers (Westminster, MD: Newman Press, 1957) p. 92.

9.   St. John of the Cross: *The Spiritual Canticle,* op.cit., p. 538.

10.   St. Bernard: Sermon 30, 6; *On the Song of Songs* II, trans. Kilian Walsh, O.C.S.O. (Kalamazoo MI: Cistercian Publications, 1976) pp. 116-117.

11.   Cf. Is 58:10; Ps 37:6; Jb 11:17; Prv 4:18.

12.   Cf. Marvin H. Pope: *Song of Songs*, op.cit., pp. 348-350.

13.   On this point, cf. Marvin H. Pope's commentary, op.cit., pp. 368-370.

14.   Cf. the footnote in *The Jerusalem Bible*, note c, p. 995.

15.   St. John of the Cross: *The Spiritual Canticle*, op.cit., Stanza 26, p. 512.

16.   St. Ambrose on Ps. 118; cited by Fr. Juan Gonzalez Arintero, O.P.: *The Song of Songs: A Mystical Exposition*, trans. James Valender and Jose L. Morales (Cincinnati, OH: Monastery of the Holy Name, 1974) p. 237.

17.   Origen: *Commentary on the Song of Songs*, op.cit., Book Three, p. 234

18.   St. Augustine: *Meditations*, ch. 2 cited by Fr. Juan Gonzalez Arintero, op.cit., p. 255.

19.   Cf. footnote *q* in *The New Jerusalem Bible* (N.Y.: Doubleday, 1966) p. 163 as a comment to Jn 7:38. It reads: "From Jesus himself, according to the oldest tradition, though another has joined 'the man who believes in me' with what follows making the 'streams' flow from the believer."

20.   On this point, see the excellent presentation by Hugo Rahner, S.J.: "The Beginnings of the Devotion in Patristic Times," in *Heart of the Savior*, ed. Josef Stierli (N.Y.: Herder & Herder, 1957) pp. 37-57.

21.   St. John Chrysostom, cited by H. Rahner, op.cit., p. 54.

22.   St. Bernard, op.cit., Sermon 75, *PL*, Vol. 183, no. 1, 1144C.

23.   St. John of the Cross: *The Dark Night of the Soul*, op.cit., I, 9,2.

24.   T.S. Eliot: *Four Quartets* (N.Y.: Harcourt & Brace & Co., 1943) p. 39.

25. M. Pope, op.cit., pp. 436-437.

26. Many early translations, following the Septuagint, such as the Vulgate, Syriac and Arabic, as well as Martin Luther's, have in place of *love* "your breasts." This ushered in many bizarre interpretations within the Christian tradition.

27. St. John of the Cross: *The Spiritual Canticle*, op.cit., Stanza 32, p. 534.

28. St. John of the Cross: *The Spiritual Canticle*, op.cit., Stanza 17, p. 480.

29. *The Way of the Pilgrim* in G.P. Fedotov: *A Treasury of Russian Spirituality* (New York: Sheed & Ward, 1948) p. 310.

30. St. John of the Cross: *The Dark Night*, op.cit., Bk. 2, ch. 3, p. 333.

31. St. John of the cross: *The Living Flame of Love*, op.cit., Stanza 2, pp. 578-579.

32. St. Ambrose: Psalm 118, *PL*, Vol.15, 1382 B.

33. St. Bernard: *Sermo 69* on the *Song of Songs*, PL, Vol.183, 1112C.

34. Many modern commentators dispute whether the author actually compared her to Tirzah and Jerusalem. In Ugaritic Usage, *ktrsh* would derive from the verb *tirzeh*, meaning "thou art pleasing," The translation offered would read: "Fair you are, my darling, verily pleasing; beautiful, awesome as (with) trophies." Cf. M. Pope, op.cit., pp. 559-560.

35 On a long and learned dissertation of the meaning of the Hebrew word 'egoz, meaning generically *nut* and specifically *walnut*, cf. op.cit., pp. 574-579.

36. Cf. M. Pope, op.cit., pp. 617ff.

37. St. John of the Cross: *The Spiritual Canticle*, Stanza 27,6, pp. 518-519, op.cit.

38. St. Teresa: *Interior Castle*, trans. E. Allison Peers (Garden City, N.Y.: Doubleday Image Books, 1961 edition) Ch. 3, p. 219.

39. St. John of the Cross: *The Spiritual Canticle*, op.cit., Stanza 37, 7, p. 552.

40. St. John of the Cross: *The Living Flame of Love*, op.cit., Stanza 1:3, p. 580.

41. St. Symeon the New Theologian: Hymn 25 in *Hymns of Divine Love by St. Symeon the New Theologian*, trans. George A. Maloney, S.J., pp. 135-136 (Denville, N.J.: Dimension Books, 1975).

42. I have followed as the basic translation and division of the *Song* which are given in *The Jerusalem Bible* (Garden City, N.Y.: Doubleday & Company, Inc., 1966). The editors of this translation give Chapter 8:7b through verse 14 in appendices, while translations that rely directly on the Jewish Massoretic text or the Septuagint Greek versions place these as the concluding verses of the *Song*. I prefer to see these verses as not integral to the original text of the *Song*. In fact, they lessen the impact of the conclusion. It is the scholarship of André Robert and his students, R. Touney and A. Feuillet, that convinces me to see these verses as additions, appended centuries after the original date of composition, which A. Robert puts as around the end of the end of the 5th Century B.C.

For his excellent and scholarly treatment of the composition and structure of the *Song*, cf. A. Robert, R. Tourney, A. Feuillet: *Le Cantique des Cantiques, Traduction et Commentaire*, in the series: *Etudes Bibliques* (Paris: Librairie Lecoffre, 1963).

A. Robert's breakdown of the verses 7b through 14 is as follows:

Aphorisms of a sage (VIII, 7b)

Appendices (VIII, 8-14).

Two epigrams (VIII, 8-12).
Useless precautions (VIII, 8-10).

The two Solomons (VIII, 11-12).
Last additions (VIII, 13-14).
Prayer to Wisdom (VIII, 13).
Response to Wisdom (VIII, 14).

He argues that verse 7b comes from some sage as an aphorism that should not be a part of the authentic text, since it is impossible to arrange it in any suitable form of poetic symmetry or parallelism (pp. 306-307).

Robert asks whether the final verses, 8-14, are truly authentic to the original text and offers four arguments for rejecting them and placing them as appendices. For him there is no intelligible connection with the antecedent context. The persons introduced are not those of the Canticle. The tone has changed. The verses are either prose or defective in meter. His interpretation is that the brothers of Jerusalem are the Sadducees of the time of John Hyrcanus (135-105). The silver alludes to the three thousand talents which Hyrcanus robbed from the tomb of David. Verse 10 attests to the Pharisees' blind confidence in divine care for them against Hasmonean policy in keeping with prophetic tradition (pp. 308-329).

43. Maisie Ward: *The Divine Eccentric* (London:Sheed & Ward, 1943) p. 74.

44. St. Teresa of Avila: *Interior Castle*, op.cit., p. 214.